MAW

JOHN 6:27
BREAD OF LIFE

Christ Above All

8½ ft ft

21 =4 b 4

Christ Above All

Robert C. Shannon

STANDARD PUBLISHING
Cincinnati, Ohio   29-03194

Library of Congress Cataloging-in-Publication Data

Shannon, Robert 1930-
  Christ above all / Robert C. Shannon.
    p. cm.
  ISBN 0-87403-568-6
    1. Jesus Christ—Biography—Sermons. 2. Christian
  biography—Palestine—Sermons. 3. Sermons, American.
  I. Title.
  BT306.3.S52 1989
  232.9'01—dc20   89-34115
                                                                        CIP

Expressing the views of his own heart, the author may express views
not entirely consistent with those of the publisher.

Scripture quotations marked *NIV* are from the *Holy Bible, New Interna-
tional Version,* copyright ©1973, 1978, 1984 by the International Bible
Society. Used by permission of Zondervan Bible Publishers and the
International Bible Society.

Contents

Introduction

"We preach Christ," said the apostle Paul (1 Corinthians 1:23). He spoke not only for himself but for his colleagues, Barnabas, Silas, John Mark, Timothy, Apollos, Stephanas, Achaicus, Fortunatus, and Epaphroditus.

He spoke not only for his colleagues, but for all the apostles. When Peter preached at Pentecost he didn't dwell on the phenomenon of tongues or the accusation of drunkenness; he preached Jesus of Nazareth. When Peter and John spoke at the temple gate they spoke about Jesus. It was that same Jesus they boldly presented before the council (Acts 3:20; 4:2, 10). Philip preached Christ in the city of Samaria (Acts 8:5) and preached Jesus to the Ethiopian in his chariot (Acts 8:35). Upon Saul's conversion, "straightway he preached Christ in the synagogues" (Acts 9:20). It was Jesus as Lord of all that Peter preached at Caesarea (Acts 10:36, 42). It was the Lord Jesus that nameless evangelists preached to the Greeks at Antioch (Acts 11:20). At Thessalonica Paul argued that "this Jesus, whom I preach unto you, is Christ" (Acts 17:3). At Athens "he preached unto them Jesus, and the resurrection" (Acts 17:18). At Ephesus even evil men recognized that it was Jesus whom Paul preached (Acts 19:13). To the Corinthians Paul declared his intent to preach nothing but "Jesus Christ, and him crucified" (1 Corinthians 2:2), and to the Philippians he declared his joy that "Christ is preached" (Philippians 1:15-18). He reminded the Galatians that he set forth Jesus Christ before them (Galatians 3:1). He wrote to the Romans that the "word of faith" that he preached was the Lord Jesus.

It was not just "Jesus" that they preached. It was Jesus as Lord. The title is found at least twenty times in the book of Acts.

The subject of the apostolic preaching was the Lord Jesus Christ, crucified, risen, ascended to glory and returning in judgment (Acts 10:42; 3:20, 21; Romans 2:16; 1 Corinthians 4:5; 2 Corinthians 5:10; 1 Thessalonians 1:9, 10). If the first epistle of Peter is in fact a sermon, as some suggest, the subject of that sermon is Christ. If in fact the gospel of Mark is a sermon of Peter's, the subject of that sermon is Christ. If in fact the book of Hebrews is a sermon with a personal note attached, the subject of that sermon is Christ.

The apostles did not concentrate on that one subject because they had no other possibilities. They had had a keen interest in the restoration of the kingdom to Israel, as Acts 1 shows. Yet that subject is strangely absent from their preaching. Social issues abounded: slavery, women's rights, and many others. Political issues abounded. They lived under Roman rule, in the midst of Greek customs, facing Jewish intolerance. Yet they were silent about such things. It was said of Paul that he was not a defamer of the pagan gods and goddesses (Acts 19:37). They refused to be drawn aside by any other subject, no matter how interesting or appealing.

For us, then, preaching Christ is keeping in step with the tradition of the church in the first century. It also puts us in step with the best traditions of the church in the centuries that followed. Martin Luther said that a minister should administer "nothing but Christ and the things of Christ. . . . He should preach the pure gospel, the true faith, that Christ alone is our life, our way, our wisdom, power, glory and salvation." Thomas Chalmers preached for twelve years at Kilmany, Scotland before he moved to Glasgow and to fame. He said that during the first eight years of that ministry he preached on honor, truth, and integrity, but noticed no improvement in the lives of his people.

Then he changed and began to preach Christ. He said that at once he began to notice a change in their lives. When Henry Ward Beecher began his ministry, he saw little response and few results. He turned to the New Testament to find out what the apostles preached and why they succeeded. The rest is history.

James S. Stewart wrote: "If we are not determined that in every sermon Christ is to be preached; it were better that we should resign our commission forthwith and seek some other vocation. Alexander Whyte, describing his Saturday walks with Marcus Dods, declared, 'Whatever we started off with in our conversations, we soon made across country, somehow, to Jesus of Nazareth, to His death and His resurrection, and His indwelling,' and unless our sermons make for the same goal, and arrive at the same mark, they are simply beating the air. It was a favorite dictum of the preachers of a bygone day that, just as from every village in Britain there was a road which, linking on to other roads, would bring you to London at last, so from every text in the Bible, even the remotest and least likely, there was a road to Christ."[1]

Stewart also speaks of "the commanding relevance of Jesus." Manning called preaching "a manifestation of the Incarnate Word, from the written Word, by the spoken Word." He capitalized the W when he referred to the sermon as the spoken Word, just as he did when he referred to the "Incarnate Word." But the spoken Word does not deserve that capital W unless it points the listener to Christ, the Word made flesh.

Hugh Thompson Kerr said, "We are sent not to preach sociology, but salvation; not economics but evangelism; not reform but redemption; not culture but conversion; not progress but pardon; not the social order but the new birth; not an organization but a new creation; not democracy but the gospel; not civilization but Christ."

More than seventy years ago W.J. Lhamon wrote this tribute to the apostles: "They were entirely and beneficently innocent of all speculations about monarchianism and Eutychianism and Monophysitism and Monotheletism and supralapsarianism and sublapsarianism and kenosis and the krypsis, and the *genus ideomaticum* and the *genus apostelesmaticum*, and the *genus majestaticum*, and of transubstantiation, and consubstantiation, and eternal generation, and eternal procession, and cosubstantiality and tripersonality and the *voliproesentia* or the *multivoliproesentia* . . . Oh, thank God! The apostles were beneficently innocent of all this. They were too reverent and practical to indulge in such meddlesome speculations."

In the Yale Lectures on Preaching for 1896 Henry Van Dyke said, "It is plain that the force which started the religion of Jesus was the person Jesus. Christ was His own Christianity. Christ was the core of His own gospel. . . . It was this that sent the apostles out into the world, reluctantly and hesitantly at first, then joyfully and triumphantly, like men driven by an irresistible impulse. It was the manifestation of Christ that converted them, the love of Christ that constrained them, the power of Christ that impelled them. He was their certainty and their strength. He was their Peace and their hope. For Christ they laboured and suffered; in Christ they gloried; for Christ's sake they lived and died."

Listen again to Stewart: "The unspoken cry of every gathered congregation to the preacher is not, 'Is there any bright idea from the current religious debate?' but 'Is there any word from the Lord?'—not, 'We would see what advice may be available,' but, 'We would see Jesus.'"[2]

So the sermons in this book are sermons about Christ. They fail to do justice to the subject, as all sermons must fail to do justice to such a subject. Perhaps they fail more than most. But their objective, at least, is clear. Men need to know Christ above all other persons. Preachers need to preach Christ above all other subjects. The world needs to receive Christ above all other remedies and prescriptions. May all of us who stand in the pulpit be able to say with Paul, "We preach Christ."

---

[1]James S. Stewart, *Heralds of God*. Charles Scribner's Sons, New York.

[2]James S. Stewart, *Faith to Proclaim*. Charles Scribner's Sons, New York.

Christ Above All

Since 1710, the skyline of London has been dominated by the soaring dome of St. Paul's Cathedral. On the top of the dome is a cross. So it is fair to say that for 279 years there has been a cross on the roof of London! That is one way to say that Christ is above all.

When peace was made between Argentina and Chile, they melted down the cannons of war and made a statue of Christ holding high a cross. They mounted it on the high-ranging Andes Mountains that separate those two countries. There is a cross on the roof of South America. It says dramatically that Christ is above all.

When Sir Edmund Hillary became the first person to scale Mt. Everest, he took with him to the world's highest mountain a crucifix. He left it there among the clouds of that snowy peak. There is a cross on the roof of the world! That is a symbolic way of saying that Christ is above all.

The Bible says it best. "Christ Above All" is the theme of the book of Ephesians, the book of Colossians, and the book of Philippians. It is the theme of all four Gospels. It is the triumphant theme of the book of Revelation. Nowhere is it put better than in this text:

That the God of our Lord Jesus Christ, the Father of Glory, may give unto you the spirit of wisdom and revelation in the knowledge of him: the eyes of your understanding being enlightened; that ye may know what is hope of his calling, and what the riches of the glory of his inheritance in the saints, and what is the exceeding greatness of his power to us-ward who believe, according to the working of his mighty power, Which he wrought in Christ, when he raised him from the dead, and set him at his own right hand in the heavenly places, far above all principality, and power, and might, and dominion, and every name that is named, not only in this world, but also in that which is to come: and hath put all things under his feet, and gave him to be the head over all things to the church, which is his body, the fulness of him that filleth all in all (Ephesians 1:17-23).

The text sets Christ above all powers: "Far above all principality, and power, and might, and dominion." The text sets Christ above all priorities: "and hath put all things under his feet, and gave him to be the head over all things to the church." The text sets Christ above all persons in verses 20 and 21, for God "set him at his own right hand ... [above] every name that is named."

Christ Above All Powers

In 1 Corinthians 15, as in our text, Paul says that all things are under the feet of Christ. At the Cairo Museum you may see the ornately carved footstool of King Tut. Depicted on it are all of Egypt's enemies. When Pharaoh used his footstool, his enemies were symbolically under his feet. But all things are under Christ's feet.

He is above all military power. There is no army like His army. Without weapons they conquer the world. Their strategy is love and their armament is grace. They accomplish more with the gospel than any have accomplished with guns, achieve more with the Bible than any have done with bullets, reach farther with the sword of the Spirit than any have done with the sword of carnal warfare.

He is above all economic power. Jacob Fugger was rich enough to buy the Holy Roman Empire for Charles V. Jesus had to borrow a boat to cross the sea. But His empire lasted far longer and reached much farther than that of Charles V. Croesus was rich enough to supply the pillars for the temple of Diana at Ephesus, one of the seven wonders of the world. Jesus owned neither house nor shop. Yet He is the pillar and the ground of truth and His spiritual temple has endured. The Rothschild family was rich enough to prevent wars simply by refusing to lend money to the kings of Europe. Jesus owned neither bank nor business, but "He maketh wars to cease to the end of the earth; he breaketh the bow and spear in sunder."

Christ is above all political powers. Kipling reminded us that "the captains and kings depart." A beloved hymn notes that "crowns and thrones perish, kingdoms rise and wane." Every British monarch is crowned in Westminster Abbey, before the high altar, on which are these words from the book of Revelation: "The kingdoms of this world are become the kingdom of our God and of His Christ, and He shall reign forever and ever."

Christ is above that awful final power, death. He must reign, says Paul, until He has put all enemies under His feet. The last enemy that shall be destroyed is death. Death is the monster who foils our plans and shatters our dreams. Death is the tyrant who stalks our path, clouds our days, and disturbs our nights. Death is the last enemy, but Christ is stronger than death.

Whenever Paul thought about Christ's power, he always thought about the resurrection. In our text, he emphasizes the working of God's mighty power which He wrought in Christ when He raised Him from the dead.

We have all enjoyed the beloved hymns of William J. Kirkpatrick. He wrote "Jesus Saves" and "Tis So Sweet to Trust in Jesus." One night when Mrs. Kirkpatrick retired for the evening her husband said that he was going into his study. He often worked late. It was after midnight when she awoke to find the lights in the study still burning. She found him at his desk, dead. The pencil was still in his hand. Before him were the words of a newly completed hymn, his last hymn:

Coming home, coming home,
Nevermore to roam,
Open wide Thine arms of love,
Lord, I'm coming home.

What a way to die! What a way to live! Christ's power over death is such that we need fear it no longer. It is only "coming home." A Christ with such power is larger than our problems.

We are sometimes like the little boy who was independent. He didn't want to take his father's hand when they crossed the street. "I'll hold my own hand," he said. Sometimes we foolishly try holding our own hand, but we discover soon enough that it doesn't work. Our problems are bigger than we are; but they are not larger than Christ's resources. During His earthly ministry, Jesus confronted every sort of problem—sickness, handicaps, hunger, loneliness, the threat of the elements, grief, and death itself. He proved His power was adequate for all human problems. He proves it still. It has been well said that while all of our problems may not be solved, all of them can be managed. It is Christ who enables us to manage them.

Christ Above All Priorities

They knew something about priorities in Ephesus. The great temple of Diana was there. It was one of the seven wonders of the world. The worship of Diana had made the city rich and famous. Then Paul came preaching Jesus Christ. His conversions cut severely into the idol business. You recall the account in the book of Acts, of the riot at Ephesus and the mob that set on Paul and his fellow Christians. Those Ephesian Christians had to set Christ above all other priorities. There was the priority of custom. In Ephesus, when one spoke of the old-time religion, he was not talking about Christianity. How easy it would have been to have argued that Diana was "good enough for my father and good enough for me." It was hard to go against custom, but Christ must come first.

In 1092, the Bishop of Rome chastised the Count of Flanders for un-Christian acts. Anticipating the Count's defense, he wrote:

Does thou claim to have done only what is in conformity with ancient custom in the land? Thou shouldst know, not with standing, thy Creator hath said: My name is Truth. He hath not said, My name is Custom.

They faced also the claim of family. There must have been many at Ephesus like the man who came to Jesus volunteering to follow Him as soon as he had buried his father. Because then burial was always on the day of death, we know that his father was not yet dead. He was saying, "It would break my father's heart if I adopted a new religion. But once he is gone I am ready to follow Jesus." There must have been many at Ephesus who were tempted to say that, but Christ had to be put above family.

They faced the claim of wealth. How powerful the labor movement is in the world today. How powerful the business community is in the world today. They were equally powerful then, and they were united in their opposition to Christianity. Huge investments were at stake. Men's jobs were at stake. Many must have suffered financial loss because of Him, but they knew Jesus had prior claim. Someone has said that if your Christianity has never cost you anything, you may not have any.

There is the elementary need to simply make a living. "A person has to live," is the excuse we often give for our little compromises. They could have made that excuse at Ephesus, but Christ took priority over making a living.

We are sure that Christ must take first priority in our lives. God has already made Him head over the church. We have always argued that just as a human body can have only one head, so the church can have only one head. In theory, we are perfectly willing to let Christ be the sole head of the church. In practice, we have a bit more difficulty. If Christ is truly to be head of the church then He must come before my pet projects. How readily we assume that our own programs are the will of God. The natural result of such a view is to suppose that those who are not in favor of our projects are opposing God. But Christ must come before our personal aims and our private ambitions. He stands above all priorities.

When we have prayed, "Thine is the kingdom," has it occurred to us that such a phrase stands over against "Mine is the kingdom?" That's what many have been saying: "Mine is the kingdom." The man who decreed dogmas others must believe, doctrines others must accept, disciplines others must obey, is saying, "Mine is the kingdom." The assembly that decides ritual or right and wrong by majority vote is saying, "Mine is the kingdom." The person whose pet project must become the program of the church, the one who says, "my way or no way," the one who confuses his own plans with evangelism, his own ideas with the gospel, and his own little circle with the church is saying, "Mine is the kingdom." They are saying it so loudly they cannot hear God declaring, "This is my beloved Son, hear ye *Him!*"

Christ Above All Persons
Jesus stands taller than all other personalities of history. It is a self-evident truth that there is none like Him, "no, not one." He stands alone among the long train of history's great. The libraries of the world are filled with volumes attesting to His greatness. "Jesus," said Emerson, "whose name is not so much written as ploughed into the history of the world." Robert Spear said of Him, "It is not enough to say that the central things of Christianity is Christ. Christ is not only the center. He is also the beginning and the end. He is all in all." Moody's word was equally emphatic: "He is all in all or he is nothing at all."

Hadrian was one of the greatest Roman emperors. He built palaces, temples, and monuments all over the Roman world. Jesus put not one stone upon another, yet He left a far more indelible mark. Alexander the Great conquered the whole of the eastern Mediterranean world. On and on his armies swept from victory to victory. He died as Jesus did at age thirty-three. Yet Alexander's kingdom did not last as long as it took to win it. Christ's kingdom endures still!

He is above all persons because of His deity. There have been great prophets and great priests and great kings. Sometimes you find two of those offices combined, as with the priest-kings in the days of the Maccabees, but only Christ is prophet, priest, and king. All other prophets said, "That is the way." Jesus said, "I am the way." All other priests came often with the blood of animals. Jesus came once for all with His own blood and entered the Most Holy Place. All other kings hoped to see their sons sit upon the throne when they were gone. His is an eternal kingdom and He reigns forever and ever.

Once the Hapsburgs ruled half of Europe. Their domain included Germany, Switzerland, Austria, and Italy. Today, one Hapsburg monarch still stands as king—Prince Franz Joseph II, who rules tiny Liechtenstein, only sixty-one square miles, the fourth smallest country in the world. The reign of Christ grows larger with each succeeding generation, and so it will continue until time is no more.

Christ is above all persons in His wisdom. Wisdom and power are key words in this chapter. God's wisdom and insight are shared with us through Christ. That wisdom must determine our course. Christ shines forth as the greatest of all teachers and so stands above our opinions, our parties, our platforms and our partitions.

I do not have a brother in the flesh, but I have a sister. We do not always agree. She does not accept some of my opinions, great as they are! But we still are brother and sister. The tie of blood is stronger than the tie of opinion.

I have many spiritual brothers. We do not always agree, but the ties of blood are stronger than the ties of opinion. We must all do homage to the one infallible teacher, Christ. When we use the hymn "Blest Be the Tie That Binds," we ought to capitalize the "T" in "Tie." Christ is the Tie that binds our hearts in Christian love. It is not emotions, nor ideas, nor opinions. It is Christ who draws us together, as verse 10 emphasizes. If we cry "heresy" at the drop of an opinion, even a tentative one, we make ourselves a laughingstock to the world and we bring pain to Christ. Have you ever tried to fathom the intricate divisions of Islam or Buddhism? They are so subtle no outsider can understand them. If we likewise appear incomprehensible to the world, they will not give us a hearing.

In 1869, Isaac Errett, who founded Standard Publishing, wrote:

It is fatal to assume that we have certainly learned all that the Bible teaches. This has been the silly and baneful conceit of all that have gone before us. Shall we repeat the folly and super-induce a necessity for another people to be raised up to sound a new battle cry for reformation?

Christ, then, stands above the claims and the counterclaims of a divided Christendom. He stands as well above the confusion of a troubled world.

In Philippians 2:9 and in our text we see this emphasis upon Christ as the one whose name is above every name. Thus Christ stands above all persons. He is above angelic persons. In Hebrews it is written, "being made so much better than the angels, as he hath by inheritance obtained a more excellent name than they." He is above demonic persons. There is much emphasis these days upon the subjects of the devil and demon possession. Such studies must not distract us from Christ. We dare not become more interested in the Antichrist than we are in the Christ, more enthralled by the second coming than we are by the first, more informed about His return than we are about His redemption, more expert in eschatology than we are in Christology.

You can draw a much bigger crowd if you announce a study of Revelation than you can if you announce a study in the life of Christ, but the latter will be far more productive.

He is above all spiritual persons. From time to time, there recurs an emphasis on the Holy Spirit; but Christ is the heart of the gospel. The Holy Spirit inspired Paul to write to the Colossians that in all things Christ is to have the preeminence. It is a shame that in some quarters the dove has replaced the cross. The change in symbols is terribly significant. The Holy Spirit did not die for you! Only Jesus saves! The Holy Spirit convicts, but Jesus saves! The church proclaims, but Jesus saves! Man witnesses, but Jesus saves!

Look at the scene in Heaven described in Revelation 5:

And I beheld, and I heard the voice of many angels round about the throne, and the beasts, and the elders: and the number of them was ten thousand times ten thousand, and thousands of thousands; saying with a loud voice, Worthy is the Lamb that was slain to receive power, and riches, and wisdom, and strength, and honor, and glory, and blessing. And every creature which is in heaven, and on the earth, and under the earth, and such as are in the sea, and all that are in them, heard I saying, Blessing, and honor, and glory, and power, be unto him that sitteth upon the throne, and unto the Lamb forever and ever (Revelation 5:11-13).

He is above all human persons. He is above all princes, popes, and potentates, above all bishops and superintendents, above all preachers and teachers, above all editors and elders. He is above all persons. That must mean that He is above me! There's the rub! I can put Him above prophets. I can put Him above priests. I can put Him above kings. I can put Him above government. I can put Him above wealth. I can put Him above the church. But can I put Him above me? That's the challenge of the hour. That's the challenge of this text. And that's the challenge of William Cowper's beloved hymn:

The dearest idol I have known,
Whate'er that idol be;
Dear Lord, I tear it from my heart
And worship only Thee.

Jesus, the Light of the World

"Light!" It's there on the first page of the Bible when God created the heavens and the earth. "Light!" It's there on the last page of the Bible when God created the new Heaven and the new earth and said, "the lamb is the light thereof." And it is here on the first page of the Gospel of John:

> In him was life, and that life was the light of men. The light shines in the darkness, but the darkness has not understood it . . . He was in the world, and though the world was made through him, the world did not recognize him. He came to that which was his own, but his own did not receive him (John 1:4, 5, 10, 11, *NIV*).

Here we see the universal light that lights every man that comes into the world. Here we see the rejected light that world would not receive.

If you've ever traveled through the tobacco-growing regions, you've seen the little buildings in which they grade the leaves of tobacco. They are all situated so that their windows face north. Before the advent of the fluorescent tube, the only true light was the north light. The delicate shades of color could not be distinguished in any light except that true light. Before the fluorescent tube, diamonds were always judged by light that came from a window facing the north. Only the true light could show the color and clarity without distortion.

Christ is the light of the world. He is the true light. Other lights shine in the world, but they are not the true light. There is the light that comes to us from the book of knowledge. We would not want to be without that light. It blesses us and helps us in many ways. But that is a light that is continually changing. If you have an encyclopedia that is twenty years old, it's out of date. If you have a science book that is ten years old, it's out of date. If you have a computer book that is five years old, it's out of date. We have to keep revising the book of knowledge and updating it. It is not the true light.

Logic is not the true light. If you live your life by logic, you'll never be happy. You'll never know love. You'll never give anything to anybody. You'll never know kindness or generosity. There is no logic in these deeds. He who lives life simply by logic finds life to be barren and sterile. Logic is not a true light.

The example of others is not a true light. There are good people who will set a good example all of their lives and then in one single moment they will set a bad example. If all you have to follow is human example, you will find it unreliable.

We need the true light; the light that never flickers. Have you ever tried to read a newspaper by the flashing light of a neon sign? Off. On. Off. On. It's a very frustrating thing. But Christ offers a light that never flickers. His is a light that never fails. It doesn't just shine for a while and then disappear. It doesn't grow dimmer and dimmer. Indeed, it's quite the opposite. It grows brighter and brighter. His is a light that never distorts. It shows things as they truly are. It shows the real colors of life.

In Fort Myers, Florida you can see the home of Thomas Alva Edison. Depicted there is the long struggle that brought at last the incandescent bulb and electric light to the world. How hard he had to work! How long he had to persevere! How great were the difficulties! But he kept at it until the job was done.

The search that we make for the true spiritual light is equally long and difficult. When we find that true light we rejoice in the light.

The light is the life of men. It's the true light. It's the light that lights every person who comes into the world. It's the universal light: a light for all people, kindreds, tongues, and nations. Whatever the land of their origin, whatever the language they speak, whatever the shade of their skin, whatever the cultures or customs with which they are familiar, whatever the structure of the body or the face, they need the true light. It is not enough to give them the sayings of Confucius, the statues of Buddha, the idols of Hinduism, the shrines of Shintoism, or the scrolls of Judaism. They must have more than that. On whatever continent or island they live, they need Jesus, the light of the *world!*

A lot of people don't believe that! We won't argue with them. They can take their argument up with Jesus, who said, "Go into *all the world* and preach the gospel to every creature." He is the light that lights every man who comes into the world. He is the universal light.

It's a light for all persons. It's a light for all situations. What is your situation today? Is it a time of success or a time of failure? Is it a time of abundance or a time of want? Is it a time of health or a time of illness? Is it a time of joy or a time of sorrow? Is it a time when you're weighed down by sin or is it a time when you are challenged by holy ideals? What is the situation of your life? Whatever it is, Jesus brings light to your situation. He may not take you out of it, but He will give you the light that you may see your way through it. No light shines farther and no light travels faster.

Light is infinite in its scope. It's the ultimate. There is nothing like it. It reaches out as far as the mind of man can reach. Light travels at 186,000 miles per second! That's faster than our fastest jet! That's faster than our mightiest rocket!

We know of nothing that travels as fast as light, except Jesus, the light of the world. All you have to do is pray and He is there. Seek His name and He is present. Invoke His power and you have it.

Nothing travels faster than light. Nothing travels farther than light. If you were to measure the distance of the twenty nearest stars (not counting our sun), they are only twelve light-years away. You take the distance light travels in a second, then multiply it by the number of seconds in a year. Twelve times the distance light travels in a year is the distance of some of the closest stars. If one of them went out tonight, you'd notice it in about twelve years. Those are the *near* neighbors. Out on the fringes of the universe there are stars that are 6,000,000,000 light-years away.

From beyond the farthest fringe of the universe Jesus comes! Into our universe! Into our solar system! Unto our earth! Into our lives! None travels faster and none travels farther.

Yet we regard light as such a commonplace thing. And we take Jesus, the light of the world, so much for granted. But when we talk about light and when we talk about Christ, we are talking about the two ultimates of our knowledge. The ultimate of the material universe and the ultimate in spiritual understanding!

Light is the ultimate in life itself. Without light there is no life. It is the ultimate in speed and power. Christ is 'the ultimate' spiritually.

Light is the ultimate in beauty. The Dutch artists were the first to try to put light on canvas. They tried to paint so the light seemed to come from within the painting itself. They were masters at it. It is thought that they developed it because the light shines so peculiarly in Holland. Surrounded by the sea, almost always covered by a mass of clouds, the light filters through and shines in a very striking and unique way that is not the same anywhere else on earth. Seeing that beauty, those Dutch artists tried to capture it and put on canvas the beauty of light.

Jesus, the light of the world, shines in the splendor of His glory and His beauty.

Light purifies. Before we had all our modern germ-killers the only way to purify a thing was to hang it out in the sunlight. That's why we sing, "Walking in Sunlight" and "Stepping in the Light."

Light is our security. That's why we light our streets and our homes.

Light cheers us. That's universal. When the sun shines people feel better. When there are weeks without sun they get depressed.

Jesus cheers us. The Bible says, "The disciples were glad when they saw the Lord." Jesus said, "Be of good cheer."

Light cures us. Now the laser, a beam of light, has become the newest surgical tool of modern medicine. "In him was light and the light was the life of men."

Light to purify. Light to give us security. Light to cheer us. Light to cure us.

Now here's something very surprising! Some reject the light! They reject its cheer. They reject its protection. They reject its purification. They reject its power. There are some who reject the light!

Some of them reject it because they cannot agree on the nature of Jesus. As scientists once argued over the nature of light, so people argue now over the nature of Jesus. Once people said light was made up of particles. Other people said light was made up of waves. The battle raged until now it is admitted that light has some of the properties of each.

So people argue over Jesus. They ask, "Who is He? Is He man or Messiah? Is He human or divine? Is He teacher or Lord? Is He son of man or Son of God?

The light is rejected in spite of the fact that the psalmist said, "The Lord is my light and my salvation." The light is rejected in spite of the fact that the prophet said, "The Lord shall be for you an everlasting light." The light is rejected in spite of the fact that Jesus, for His text in His hometown of Nazareth, chose a verse from Isaiah that said, "The Spirit of the Lord is upon me . . . [to preach] the recovering of sight to the blind" (Luke 4:18).

John continues this theme, "Jesus the Light." He begins in chapter 1. In chapter 8, verse 12 he quotes Jesus, "I am the light of the world." Notice the universal side to that! "I am the light of the world: he that followeth me shall not walk in darkness." Again in chapter 9, verse 5, "As long as I am in the world, I am the light of the world."

Again in chapter 12, verse 36, "While ye have light, believe in the light that ye may be the children of light." The saddest of all is in chapter 3, verse 20, "For everyone that doeth evil hateth the light, neither cometh to the light, lest his deeds should be reproved."

That's why men reject the light. That's why they turn to darkness. Their deeds are evil and they do not want them reproved!

I learned in Africa that when you go as a guest to a mission station, the first question you ask is, "What time does the generator go off?" Because at some predetermined time in the evening every light is going to go out. When it goes out it is not going to come on again until darkness falls the following evening. You don't want to be in the middle of something that you can't finish in the dark.

We need the light and we cherish the light, unless our deeds are evil. Then we shun the light and we cherish the darkness.

The history of man's search for light is long. He began depending solely on daylight and when darkness fell, he could no longer work. Then man discovered fire. He could bring that flickering light into his cave. Then he devised the candle. After that, the lamp. Finally, electricity and the incandescent light. Then the neon lamp. Then the fluorescent light. Now fiber optics can carry your telephone message on a beam of light. Lasers can do surgery with a beam of light. Who would want to abandon all of that and go back to a firelight flickering in a cave or only to the light of day?

Yet men do turn back to darkness and turn away from the light. They say that the darkness is fine for them. Well, that may be all right for the way they live, but it's not going to be all right when they die. They're going to cry out with the dying German poet Goethe, "Light. More light."

That's what we need for life. That's what we need for death. And that's what we can have in eternity.

We know him as O. Henry. His real name was William Sydney Porter. When he lay dying, he called out to his nurse, "Pull up the shades, Mary. I'm afraid to go home in the dark."

Are you going to go home in the dark or in the light?

Jesus, the Lamb of God

Seldom do you know the end of a book from the beginning. Never do you know the end of a life from the beginning. Who would put the conclusion right alongside of the introduction? John does.

In the first chapter of his Gospel, the 29th verse, John the apostle quotes John the Baptist, who, seeing Jesus come to him, said, "Behold the Lamb of God, which taketh away the sin of the world!"

There you have the conclusion of Jesus' life at the very introduction of Jesus' ministry. You know from the beginning what the end is going to be.

They understood John's words, but they could not appreciate their meaning and they forgot them. But it was there at the very start.

Did you know at the beginning of your life how it was going to turn out? Of course not. Very few of us imagined that we would be in this place at this point in our lives. We didn't know whom we would marry, what our career might be, where life might take us. But Jesus from the very beginning of His ministry knew what the end was going to be.

The word "behold" is a word we trip over all to lightly when we read the Bible. It's intended to spotlight something. It's intended to draw our attention to something. The word "behold" means something like "Look here! See this!" We know that something very astonishing is going to be laid out before us.

So, in this single verse, this single truth, there are three startling aspects. First, we see how startling it is that a man should take the place of a lamb. Second, we are startled to learn that the offended should provide the atonement for the offender. Third, it startles us to know that one deed by one man can erase many deeds done by many men.

"Behold the Lamb of God, that taketh away the sin of the world." A man takes the place of a lamb! They understood that because they were familiar with lambs and their relationship to sin. In fact, they knew all along that a lamb could take the place of a man. So, it is rather startling to see the opposite.

They began with that at birth. It was a law of the Jews that the firstborn belonged to God. But all human sacrifice was prohibited. How could you give the firstborn to God and make no human sacrifice? You had a substitute. A lamb took the place of a man. That was at their very birth.

It carried them back in memory to when their ancestors were in Egypt and God said, "I'm going to pass through Egypt and I'm going to slay the firstborn in every household." But to the Jews he said, "If you will kill a lamb and put the blood on the doorpost, then the lamb will take the place of the man. I will not slay the firstborn in your household."

They understood its relationship to sin. Whenever they sinned, they brought an offering to the Lord—a lamb. They knew that "the soul that sinneth, it shall die." But they brought the lamb instead. Before their altars the lamb took the place of the man.

Standing on that vast paved courtyard that once housed the temple of the living God, one might think about all of the feet that had passed that way. Solomon in all his splendor built this temple. There were the priests and the Levites who had come that way. Jesus' feet passed over those stone! Strangely, we might be most impressed not by these, but by the cloven feet that by the thousands had walked in this place the lambs sacrificed for the sake of Israel, sacrificed for the sins of Israel.

John the Baptist was familiar with all of this because he belonged to the priestly family. His father had killed those lambs and laid them on the altar. He had seen it done over and over again. Because of his rich familiarity with their custom, he saw it as an illustration of a new striking truth. So, he turned the whole thing upside down. Often lambs had taken the place of men, now a man would take the place of a lamb.

John the Baptist could have introduced Jesus to the world as a lion rather than a lamb. The lion is as prominent in prophecy as the lamb. The coming Messiah is described as "the Lion of the tribe of Judah."

Did you ever play that little parlor game where you decide what animal you would like to be? Somebody says, "A bird, so I can soar through the heavens." Somebody says, "A race horse, beautiful and graceful." Somebody says, "An owl, because he is wise." Or, "A turtle, because he lives so long." Or, "A lion, because he is the king of the jungle." But who wants to be a lamb?

John the Baptist could very well have introduced Jesus to the world as the lion of God. It's true and it's scriptural. But he chose instead to introduce Jesus to the world as the Lamb of God. There is a reason behind that choice, just as there was a reason behind all of those sacrifices. Look at them superficially and it's utterly incomprehensible. Does God love to see animals die? Does He rejoice in the shedding of blood? Do the pain and the death mean something to Him? How strange! How macabre!

No, it all looks to the future. Without the sacrifice of those lambs, we would not have the striking contrast of this text. The only way that we ever understand anything is by comparing it with something or contrasting it with something. When we want to describe something we say, "It's just like . . ." Or we say, "It's just the opposite of . . ." That's the only way we ever understand anything—comparison, contrast. Without all those tens of thousands of lambs on the altar of Israel, we could never understand what Jesus came to do.

In our own experience an animal takes the place of a man. If we want to experiment with drugs or surgical procedures, what do we do? We take an animal. Some people are opposed to that.

29

They are not thinking it through. We don't favor cruelty to animals, but on the other hand, we must test our drugs and we must test our procedures. Shall we test them on a human or shall we test them on an animal? The answer's obvious. It would be better for 10,000 mice to have cancer if a cure for cancer for people could thereby be found.

So, for an animal to take the place of a man is not only a part of Israel's experience, but it's a part of our experience, and not just in the world of research. Until recent times on a farm an animal took the place of a man. An animal carried the burden. An animal pulled the load. An animal pulled the plow. It's a principle with which we are thoroughly familiar. How startling to see it suddenly turned upside down.

We say the value of a man is far greater than the value of an animal. But what is the value of a man? This is a question that comes up in Scripture. At the time of Joseph a man was worth twenty pieces of silver. That's what Joseph's brothers got for him when they sold him into slavery. By the time Jesus came along inflation had taken its toll; Judas got thirty pieces of silver for Jesus.

When the Nazis occupied Holland, many of the Dutch hid Jews from Nazis to save their lives. The Nazis, in order to counteract that, offered a reward for every Jew who was turned in— 7½ gilders. That's what they said a man was worth.

The worth of a man! That's a thought to ponder. We are worth so much that Jesus would come and take the place of a lamb for the sake of man.

If we are startled to see a man take the place of a lamb, we're startled all the more to see that the offended provided the atonement for the offender.

How surprised his audience must have been when John the Baptist said, "the Lamb of God." Wait a minute! God hasn't sinned. Why does God need a lamb? Man needs a lamb. Man has sinned. God is holy. God is righteous and just. God has never sinned. What do you mean, "the Lamb of God?"

Such questions must have arisen in their minds. It is as if a thief should rob you, be caught, tried, and convicted, and then you have to serve his sentence. There's not one of us who would do that.

We are certain that it is the offender who must make tion, not the one who has been offended—the guilty and n innocent, the wounder and not the wounded.

That's the way we think it is in the family. Mother says to the little child who has just beaten up on the sibling, "You go and say you're sorry." The one who has been beaten up doesn't have to say anything. It's the one who has done the deed that must say, "I'm sorry" and make restitution.

There were once two brothers who didn't speak. Each one said, "I'm perfectly willing to patch up the quarrel, but it isn't my fault. It's the other one who has done the injury and he is the one who must come and say he is sorry. I'm perfectly willing to forgive him as soon as he admits he is wrong."

That's the way we operate in life. That's the way we operate in society. In the little insults that come to us and the little hurts and grievances, we say, "All right! That person hurt me! That's the person who must begin to make restitution."

That's the way it is in law. The law doesn't fine the person who has been damaged by the crime. The law fines the criminal.

That's the way it is in nature. If you offend the laws of electricity, it will not be your next-door neighbor who will be electrocuted! If you offend the laws of poison, it will not be your next-door neighbor who will be rushed to the emergency room.

So, here is a principle that runs all the way through the world. There are very few exceptions to it. There is one in the Old Testament.

Hosea's wife had left him. She had been more than unfaithful to him. She had actually become a prostitute. She had gotten down to the lowest rank of prostitute and was living in the slums of the city. Hosea, who had been wounded, searched for her and found her. He pleaded with her to come back. All along we think that she should have pleaded with him to *take* her back.

It also happened in the New Testament as God, the offended, provided the sacrifice for the offender.

We're glad that He did because He alone could do it. We had nothing to give in expiation for our sins. Our sins are too vast and too numerous. If He had not done it, it could not have been done at all.

A frequent blood donor, a preacher, went to the Adler building in Clearwater, Florida where the blood bank is located. He drove a Volkswagen. He pulled his battered ten-year-old Volkswagen into the parking lot and there sat a magnificent new Rolls Royce. That Rolls Royce cost more than his entire net worth. He knew whose it was because the parking space was marked *Edward Adler*. He knew that that Rolls Royce belonged to the wealthy couple who had given an enormous amount of money to build that building to house a blood bank. Without a moment's hesitation he parked his little VW right beside the Rolls Royce. He knew that his contribution was just as necessary as theirs. You cannot transfuse dollars into veins. All they had given would be worthless without people of another rank coming in to give blood.

No other person could have made the atonement if God had not provided it through Christ.

In the city of Thessalonica in Greece there is a church called the church of St. Demetrius. In the church there is a box. In the box there is a handful of earth. They say this was soaked with the blood of St. Demetrius when he died as a Christian martyr. We are never to take martyrdom lightly, but the blood of St. Demetrius cannot do for you what the blood of Jesus can do for you!

There is something else startling in this text. That is that one deed done by one man on one day should erase many deeds done by many men. That's not logical. Logic tells you just the opposite. Logic tells you that for one sin you ought to do a whole lot of good deeds. Maybe a whole lot of good deeds will overbalance the one sin. Logic tells you that while many good deeds might erase one bad deed, obviously, one good deed could not logically erase many evil deeds.

There is much in the world that is not logical. It is not logical that we should be loved, but it is true. It is not logical that our mates should love us. It is not logical that our children should honor us, but they do. It is not logical that our friends should be loyal to us, but they are. There is a great deal in the world that is true, but is not logical. Here is something that is absolutely true and totally illogical: one deed done by one person, Jesus Christ, can erase many deeds done by many persons.

It would have been amazing if this text had taught that Jesus in a single act erased all of *my* sins. It would have been amazing if this text had taught us that Jesus in a single act erased all of the sins of the people in one city. It would have been amazing if the text had taught us that Jesus in a single deed managed to erase all the sins that Americans had ever committed, or all the sins of the twentieth century. But it's larger than that. It's the sin of the world!

It's not logical but it is true. It's not limited but it is universal. It's not limited to geography. It's not limited to race. It's not limited to financial status. It's not limited to education. It's not limited to social standing. It's not limited to anything!

It's not logical, but true. It's not limited, but universal. It's not automatic, but it is conditional.

There was once a man who never went to church. Somebody told him that he ought to go to church. He asked, "Why? Jesus died for everybody's sins, so he died for mine. I don't have to bother about it." He didn't understand that universal doesn't mean automatic.

Jesus will never forgive you of the sin of which you do not repent! Not in this world and not in the next! He will never forgive you if you do not believe. That's the foundation stone of forgiveness and salvation. It's absolutely necessary.

It must be a personal thing. He will not forgive you on the grounds that your wife has faith, or your husband has faith, or your parents have faith, or your children have faith. It must be a heartfelt faith, a confessed faith, an obedient faith.

Jesus said that those who rejected the baptism of John the Baptist rejected the counsel of God. What would He say of those who reject the baptism that He himself commanded?

Faith: personal, heartfelt, confessed, obedient. That's what it takes if the blood is to be applied.

The Lamb appears 27 times in the book of Revelation. Most often he's on a throne! It's the *Lamb* who is on the throne in Heaven. But though the Lamb is on the throne and the blood dried in the dust of Calvary long ago, still the blood avails. Still the death has power for life. Still the Lamb takes away si~

Dear dying Lamb, the precious blood
Shall never lose its power
Till all the ransomed Church of God
Be saved to sin no more.
                    (Cowper)

The Uplifted Christ

Hear the word of the Lord in John 12:32. "And I, if I be lifted up from the earth, will draw all men unto me."

All men! Rich, poor, educated, ignorant, old, young, black, white, cultured, crude! "I will draw all men unto me."

What an audacious statement that is! No one would believe it of course, unless history had proved it true. But now with all these centuries between this text and our time, no one can dispute it. No one can deny it. The long centuries of church history have proved that it is absolutely true! We don't need to defend this text.

There are two sides to it: the magnetism of the cross and the manner in which Christ is lifted up. We will begin with the second.

The text leaves no doubt as to the manner. John adds after this text, "This he said, signifying what death he should die." Jesus was talking about the cross when He said, "If I'm lifted up, I'll draw all men to me."

Christ was lifted up upon a cross. He knew how He was going to die. We don't know how early He knew it. In Bethlehem is the Church of the Nativity. Over the place where it is thought the manger stood is a tapestry. Woven into the tapestry is a cross.

The shadow of the cross was indeed over the cradle of Christ. When His parents took the infant Christ to the temple, Simeon the prophet spoke of a sword of sorrow that would pierce the heart.

To suppose that Jesus in His childhood or youth was thinking of the cross would be a heartless supposition. Yet surely when His ministry began, at least from that point on, the shadow of the cross hung unmistakably over Him. He knew how He was going to die.

That it was a cross is perhaps coincidental. The death of Christ would have meant fully as much to the world if He had died in some other way. His blood would have been just as powerful to forgive our sins. He might have been put to death by drowning, as some of His followers were. Many Christian martyrs lost their lives in this way. When you see a baptism, remember there have been Christians who died because they believed in baptism by immersion. They were drowned. Jesus' death would have been as effective for our forgiveness if He had died in this way, or if He had been buried alive as other Christian martyrs were, or burned at the stake.

But there seems to be a special lesson in the fact that He died on a cross, lifted up, held up to public view, above the men who stood below to ridicule Him. That cross was lifted up on a hill. Jesus' death would have meant as much to the world if He had been crucified in a valley or on a plain. It is only by coincidence that the cross happened to be on a hill. Yet what an instructive coincidence that is.

When we stand on a hill, we get a better viewpoint. We can see more clearly. Is there any place on earth where we see things as clearly as at Calvary? Standing in other places our view of life is distorted and thrown out of focus. When we stand on top of that hill where Jesus died, we are able to see life clearly and to see ourselves clearly. The mists roll away. From the vantage point of Calvary we can see farther. We can see beyond the immediate things we worry about or think about. We see the ultimate things that ought to occupy our attention.

Yes, the fact that the cross was on the hill teaches us that here we have a viewpoint that we need. Standing on that "green hill far away" we have a different vantage point, too.

Before the advent of airplanes and helicopters, generals always had their battle stations on hilltops. There they could look out over the whole scene of battle. They could see how the enemy troops had been deployed. They could see where they needed to move in reinforcements or change their strategy. They could map out the whole battle plan because they had a vantage point. Men built their castles and forts on the tops of hills. They were harder to storm, easier to defend.

At Calvary we have a vantage point—a vantage point from which we as Christian soldiers can march out in His name; a vantage point from which we can plan a strategy to win the world to Christ.

He was lifted up upon a cross. The cross was lifted up upon a hill, but all of that is significant only because of who it is who hung on that cross.

Let others who will praise the cross of the Christ,
The Christ of the cross is my king.
For though we must cherish the old rugged cross,
'Tis only the Christ can redeem.

A thousand crosses had been stuck into the sand of Palestine. Jesus was neither the first nor the last to die on a cross. His cross is significant because of who He is! Here the sinless Son of God died for man. That makes all the difference.

That's the meaning of the text. The Christ, lifted up on his cross, draws all men to Him. But would we be doing that text an injustice to go a step beyond it? Since Christ has been lifted up upon that cross, He now must be lifted up before the world. He must be lifted up in worship.

In addition to the alphabetical index in the back of the hymnal there is a second index. It is a topical index. Among the categories there is one marked, "Christ." You'll discover that in the hymnal there are more songs about Christ than about any other subject. That's the way it ought to be. In worship we lift Him up!

Compare the songs that speak of our fumbling human experience and the songs that lift up Christ. Which ones inspire you more? Which ones do you more good? The songs that turn inward upon our need or situation or victory or defeat or the songs that cause us to look up to Him?

We come about the table of Communion that Christ may be lifted up. We must always see more than bread and wine. Christ is lifted up in Communion. If all else fails, if the sermon falls flat, if the songs are filled with discords and no one gives us a happy greeting, we will still find inspiration at the Communion table. Christ is lifted up in Communion.

Every time we witness a baptism we must see someone other than the preacher and the person. We must see three people there. The whole purpose of baptism is to lift up Christ. We lift Him up in worship.

We lift Him up when we preach. A wise man said to a group of ministers, "When all the rest of you are preaching up the times, I hope you will permit one poor brother to preach up Christ."

It's not the purpose of the sermon to give us *U.S. News and World Report.* We can find that at the newsstand. The sermon must tell us something that we will not read in *Time* magazine or in the daily newspaper. It is something that you will not hear on the television news. One must lift up Christ above the issues of the day that confuse us, above the problems of the hour that terrify us.

Another minister said to a group of his fellow ministers, "In every text in the Bible there is a track that leads to Christ. Find it and follow it."

Let life lift up Christ. He was lifted up upon His cross. He is lifted up in worship. He is lifted up in preaching. Let Him be lifted up in life. Let us pray that at least one time in our lives someone will see something in us that makes them think of Him; that we will do at least one deed of which someone will say, "That's what Christ would have done." Let us pray that at one point in life our response to some situation or to some individual will be the very response that Christ would have made.

It is perhaps expecting too much to suppose that would happen very often. Let us hope that it happens sometime; that life lifts Him up.

We must speak of the magnetism when Christ is lifted up. Magnets are fascinating! They were our toys when we were children. Then we learned that somebody magnetized a needle, put it in a little round box and made a compass that unerringly pointed north. Later on men discovered that you could take a coil of wire, spin it between the poles of a magnet and produce electricity.

Our buildings are lighted today by a magnet. They are cooled or heated as we desire by a magnet. All the wheels of industry are turned by a magnet.

Do you see how we have moved to succeedingly higher levels of magnetism? From the toy, to the compass, to electricity, to the universe. You might suppose that how we can go to no higher level, but such a supposition would be wrong. More powerful than the magnetism of the planets is the magnetism of Christ.

He draws us intellectually. He spoke of the deepest and profound issues of life. We do not simply discuss them in college classrooms or among professors. Children ask the same questions. Who is God? Who am I? What happens when you die? Why do people suffer? Can we be forgiven? Those are the deep issues of life and Jesus addressed them. He addressed them in terms so simple that any twelve-year-old child can understand His words, yet the wisest man among us ponders their deep meaning. He draws us intellectually.

He draws us emotionally. There is something about the great heart of Jesus that answers an emptiness in our own hearts. We wonder how anyone can love so unselfishly, so impartially, so freely, so unashamedly, so fearlessly, so sacrificially. We'd like to love like that. We'd like to love Him, and others, the way He loves us. We're drawn to Him emotionally.

We're drawn to Him spiritually. His life towers above our own. His virtues overshadow our best. We want to be more like Him.

We're drawn by His life. We're drawn by His sermons, His miracles, His feeding of the multitude, His welcoming of the children, His offer of forgiveness to the lost.

We are drawn to Jesus in His life. We are drawn most to Him in His death. Did you ever think about that strange song we sing, "Jesus, keep me near the cross"? There is something unnatural about that. Whenever we have been in the presence of death, whether at the scene of an accident or in a hospital room, our reaction has always been the same. "Let's get away from here." Why is it that we make an exception in the case of Jesus and sing, "Jesus, keep me near the cross?"

There was something different about His death, something that rises above the grim details. Preachers used to think it was effective to describe the sweat, the blood, the pain, the torn flesh. Perhaps that was not very valuable. We must see the *reason* that He died and the *Person* who died. Then we will understand the uniqueness of Jesus' death and why we are so drawn to it.

We are drawn to His cross when we need forgiveness. There is something there that answers to our need. We can believe there what we would not dare to believe in any other place: that God does, in fact, forgive sin.

We are drawn to Him on His cross when we need comfort. I had a conversation with a fellow Christian. We were discussing the meaning of suffering. I admitted that I had never experienced what this particular individual was going through. But I reminded her that Christ did understand because Christ suffered, too. The change in facial expression was like the turning on of a light. There is comfort at the cross.

When we need companionship we are drawn to the cross. Jesus suffered alone so that no one would ever have to be alone again. If any man ever is alone, it is because he chooses to be alone.

Because we are drawn to the cross, we may forget that there is another side to magnetism. A magnet has two poles. One attracts. One repels. We have read the verse that follows our text. We must now read the one that goes before it.

"Now is the judgment of this world. Now shall the prince of this world be cast out. And I, if I be lifted up from the earth, will draw all men unto me."

It is like the poles of a magnet. Christ draws some men. He repels others. But at this point the illustration runs out. The parable falls short. The analogy dies. The iron has no choice as to whether it will go to the side of the magnet that attracts or the side of the magnet that repels. You do have a choice. You can stand in that place where Christ by His divine magnetism will draw you to himself. Or you can stand at that opposite pole where Christ's magnetism repels and you are forced out into darkness and judgment.

There is only one question to ask. Where do you stand?

40

How Can I Know for Sure?

There was an old man named Zechariah. His hands had often been stained with the blood of lambs destined for the altars of Israel. His clothes had often smelled of the incense that filled that holy place. Often his feet had trod where other men dared not go—into the holy place of the temple of the Most High God. For years he had carried in his heart two hopes. The first was that he would have a son, and the second was that he would live to see the coming of the Messiah, the deliverer of Israel.

The first hope had now faded and died. The second hope was bright as ever. He was about his duties in the temple when something happened to him. It was written down in Luke 1:

Then an angel of the Lord appeared to him, standing at the right side of the altar of incense. When Zechariah saw him, he was startled and was gripped with fear. But the angel said to him: "Do not be afraid, Zechariah; your prayer has been heard. Your wife Elizabeth will bear you a son, and you are to give him the name John. He will be a joy and delight to you, and many will rejoice because of his birth, for he will be great in the sight of the Lord. He is never to take wine or other fermented drink, and he will be filled with the Holy Spirit

41

even from birth. Many of the people of Israel will he bring back to the Lord their God. And he will go on before the Lord, in the spirit and power of Elijah, to turn the hearts of the fathers to their children and the disobedient to the wisdom of the righteous—to make ready a people prepared for the Lord" (Luke 1:11-17, *NIV*).

Zechariah asked the angel, "How can I be sure of this?" That's the first of the questions of Christmas. Another is asked by Mary: "How can these things be?" Another by the wise men, "Where is he that is born?" But this is where Christmas begins, here in Luke, chapter 1, with the father of John the Baptist, Zechariah, and his probing question, "How can I be sure of this?"

Sometimes doubt asks this question. Sometimes faith asks this question. Always Christmas answers this question. In this text, it is not doubt that is asking, but faith. The difference is this. Doubt is looking for a way out. Faith is looking for a way in. Doubt is looking for a way out of the responsibilities that come with believing. Doubt is looking for a way out of the guilt that comes with believing. If for one moment I admit that Jesus is who He claims to be, if for one moment I grant His claims, then I am obligated. I am obligated to a certain way of thinking and living and doing, and people don't want that obligation. So in doubt, they say, "How can I know for sure?" Behind it all is this: they do not want to believe. That's why Jesus came down so hard on disbelief—harder than on anything else. It amazes us that Jesus should have more harsh things to say about disbelief than any other problem in life. "Woe unto thee, Chorazin," he said to one city. "Woe unto thee, Bethsaida," He said to another. "Woe unto thee, Jerusalem," He said. Again and again Jesus fiercely condemned disbelief. Why? Because people choose to doubt or they choose to believe. Doubt always has moral roots.

Whenever you meet a person who has problems with his faith, if you will probe deeply enough, you will find that he also has problems with his morals. That's where doubt begins, down in the sub-soil of life where we decide how we are going to live. Faith rises out of a determination to do right. Doubt rises out of a desire to do wrong.

42

Now because people ask out of doubt, they demand a kind of proof for Christianity that cannot be given. They demand mathematical proof of the Christian religion. You cannot prove Christianity by mathematics. Indeed, there are quite a number of important things in life that you cannot prove by mathematics. To demand mathematical proof of the Christian religion is to demand something that cannot be given.

Some people demand scientific proof of the Christian religion, but there are, after all, some things that cannot be poured into test tubes or heated over Bunsen burners or weighed on scales. Yet they are just as real as the things that can be. Bring love into your laboratory. Can you dissect or analyze it? Bring faith in. Can you dissect or analyze it? It exists in the world, whatever its basis. Some important things in the world do not lend themselves to laboratory experiments, and therefore are beyond the pale of science, as they are beyond the pale of mathematics. He who asks for that kind of proof of Christianity asks out of doubt.

Jesus illustrated the problem in the story He told about a rich man who lived in a fine house and ate sumptuously every day, and a beggar full of sores who was laid every day at his gate. The implication is that the man never thought about giving any food to the beggar and that the beggar's hunger did not diminish his appetite one bit. Death came to them both. The rich man went to Hell and Lazarus the beggar went to Heaven. In torment the rich man cried out to father Abraham, "Send Lazarus, that he may dip the end of his finger in water and cool my tongue."

Abraham said, "There's a great gulf fixed, and nobody can go from one to the other."

Then said the man, "Send him to earth, for I have five brethren. Let him testify to them lest they also come to this place of torment."

Abraham said, "They have Moses and the prophets. Let them believe them."

"No," said the man. "But if one rose from the dead, they would believe."

"No," said father Abraham, "even though one rose from the dead, they will not believe."

Now remember that it is Jesus who told us this parable. It is

Jesus who in sadness is looking ahead to His own resurrection and then looking ahead to our age, and noting that in our time, there will be people who will not believe even though He rose from the dead. The stubbornness of doubt is clearly in the mind of Jesus. Jesus understood that faith is a choice we make, and that doubt is a choice we make. People who have chosen to doubt are not going to be convinced by anything. They are going to say, "Well, how can I know for sure?"

In this text, however, the question does not rise out of doubt. It rises out of faith. Zechariah is a believer. It is faith seeking confirmation, faith seeking reassurance. What kind of confirmation does faith have a right to seek? We have already seen that it has no right to seek mathematical or scientific proof for things that are beyond the realm of mathematics and science. But faith does have a right to ask for confirmation. What men have predicted is often not confirmed by history. For example, in the early 1920s, D.W. Griffith said, "Speaking movies are impossible. When a century has passed, all thought of our so-called speaking movies will have been abandoned. It will never be possible to synchronize the voice with the picture."

In 1889, *The Literary Digest* had this piece in it. "The ordinary horseless carriage is a luxury for the wealthy. It will never, of course, come into common use as the bicycle." In 1913, a man said of the radio that it would never be possible to transmit the human voice across the Atlantic and such an idea was absurd and misleading. In 1902 Simon Newcomb, the astronomer, said, "Flight by machines heavier than air is impractical and insignificant, if not utterly impossible." Edgar Cayce, in whom some people still continue to believe, predicted an earthquake so severe that California would break off the mainland and sink into the Pacific Ocean. His followers set the date—April, 1969. It passed. They recalculated and set it for 1975. It passed. California is still here. That's the way the predictions of men work out. But if you will turn through the Bible you will find prophecy after prophecy after prophecy that came true. We have a right to expect that history will confirm Scripture, and it does.

We have a right to expect that experience will confirm our faith and reassure us. When we ask, "How can I know for sure?" we're asking experience to bear out what we've been taught.

Someone described his experience like this:

I've dreamed many dreams that never came true.
I've seen them vanish at dawn.
But I've realized enough of my dreams, thank God,
To make me keep dreaming on.

I've prayed many prayers when no answer came
Though I waited patient and long
But answers have come to enough of my prayers
To keep me praying on.

The more you pray, the more you believe in prayer. The more you pray, the more confident you are that it works. The people who doubt prayer are the people who seldom pray. The people who are confident about it are the people who pray often. God does confirm our faith and reassures us in the very experiences of life.

Suppose I were to play one of those word association games with you and say, "When I name a word, you say the first thing that comes into your mind." If I were to say the word "Ebenezer," you would say "Scrooge." That's the first thing that comes to mind at the mention of the name "Ebenezer." That's a great shame. The word "Ebenezer" is in the Bible and in the hymnal. It is in the hymnal in that song, "Here I raise my Ebenezer; Hither by Thy help I'm come." That's a reflection of a word in the Bible. It's a very important verse in the Old Testament. The Children of Israel have arrived at their destination. It has been a long and difficult journey. They put up a stone of remembrance and wrote on it, "Ebenezer." *Ebenezer* means "hitherto hath the Lord helped us." Are there not many who could write over this moment of life, "Ebenezer! Hitherto hath the Lord helped me." Experience confirms faith.

Logic confirms faith. One legend says that the wise men lost sight of the star on their journey. It faded from their view until they sought to draw water from a well and looking down into the deep well they saw the star reflected in its water. It's only a legend, but if you look into the deep things of life you will begin to see the appropriateness of Christian faith. You will see the relevance of it. You will see how it fits into our understanding of life and the world and ourselves. Yes, there is a certain logic to the Christian religion.

Zechariah did have a son. His name was John the Baptist. He was the forerunner of Christ. When Christ came on the scene, they put John the Baptist in prison. In prison, he sent his followers to ask Jesus, "Are you he that should come, or look we for another?" He was saying the same thing that his father had said, "How can I know for sure?" I preached some years ago on that text. I chose this as my title, "A Faith That Asks Questions." Many people believe that faith means not asking questions. They say, "Well, I don't question it; I just take it on faith." I'm not sure that's real faith.

Other people think that faith means having all the answers, but that's not faith either. That's knowledge. Faith means that we begin to see a glimpse of how the Christian religion fits into the fabric of all things.

The question, "How can I know for sure?" is answered in Christmas. To some people, Christmas is pure poetry. It's all romance. It's all music and candles. In the Bible, Christmas deals with the hard and sometimes harsh realities of life. Read the Christmas account in Matthew and Luke. You will find birth and death. You will find pain and loneliness. You will find travel and discomfort. You will find hunger and need. You will find misunderstanding and slander. You will find all of the harsh, hard realities of life.

Is it not appropriate that in the midst of them there should shine some light of hope? Is it not appropriate that in the darkest sky there should shine some star? Heywood Hale Broun, the famous columnist, said that one Christmas day he was at the newspaper office. Nothing is lonelier than a newspaper office on Christmas Day. The few people who had to come to work were sitting around wishing they were somewhere else. He said it was a very dull day. Then the telegraph began to click. Nobody paid much attention to it until they noticed it was clicking the same pattern over and over and over again. "Well," he thought, as he went over to the machine, "What is it? War? Peace? Death? Life?" And as he listened to the staccato ring of the telegraph key, he began to understand that the Morse Code was saying. "Unto us a child is born, unto us a child is born, unto us a child is born." Somewhere at the other end of the telegraph wire an equally bored newspaper man sat. Having nothing else to do he was tapping out over the syndicated wire the opening verses of the Christmas story. And Heywood Hale Broun said it seemed to him, in view of all of the bad news that had come across that wire, that it was singularly appropriate there should come this good news over and over again on Christmas Day, "Unto us a child is born, unto us a child is born, unto us a child is born."

What if we took Christmas out of the world and thereby take Christ out of history. I ask you what year is it and you say, "I don't know. We have no way to mark them." I ask, "Where is the hospital?" You say, "What is a hospital?" I say to you, "Direct me to the nearest church." You say, "I've never heard of that." I say, "I am in need; will you help me?" You say, "I have no time for you." Imagine—a world without Christ!

Christmas is the only festival that is not tied to the seasons. We have harvest festivals, spring festivals, midsummer festivals and midwinter festivals. We have festivals to mark birth, marriage, and coming to manhood. But Christmas stands alone, not related to the passing of the seasons and not related to the cycles of life, but utterly related to the penetrating question of the heart, "How can I know for sure?"

Christmas tells us that the report is true! The promise is kept; the presence is in our very midst. All the world stops for Christmas. Most of us will have candles. They came from Ireland. Christmas trees came from Germany. St. Nicholas came from Holland. Christmas cards came from England. Decorated houses came from Italy. Carols to sing came from Palestine and Bethlehem. All the world comes to my doorstep and all the world celebrates Christmas around my hearth. We will not hesitate to sing, "Joy to the World," written by an Independent minister, "O Little Town of Bethlehem," written by an Episcopalian, "Silent Night, Holy Night," written by a Catholic, "It Came Upon a Midnight Clear," written by a Unitarian, or "Hark the Herald Angels Sing," written by a Methodist. Something about Christmas melts away the barriers and reaches out arms of divine love to embrace the world.

If it embraces the world, it embraces me.

How Can These Things Be?

Christmas is a time for questions. Some of them are very shallow.

"What did you get for Christmas?"

"How will I ever pay for it all?"

"How can I ever get it all done?"

Some of them are not shallow at all. They are Christmas questions that arise in the Bible. "How can I know for sure?" – the question of Zechariah. "Where is He that is born?" – the question of the wise men. And this question, the question of Mary, "How can these things be?" (Luke 1:26-34)

An angel appeared to Mary and told her that she would bear a Son who would reign over the house of Jacob forever and that His kingdom would never end. She responded with the question, "How can these things be?" She responded with the voice of innocence. She responded with the voice of wonder. She responded with the voice of worship.

What is so lovely as innocence? Is there anything more beautiful? What we see here is innocence. It is not naivete. There is a vast difference between the two!

Mary was not naive. She knew how babies come into the world. She knew that in her circumstance she was not a candidate to be a mother. She was not naive, but she was innocent.

Because innocence is so rare, some believe that it does not exist at all. Disillusioned, cynical people say there really is no such thing as innocence in a person grown up and, therefore, Mary could not be innocent. For my part, I go along with Luke and the Word of God.

This innocence is set in a world of evil. It was, after all, a real world, a very real world, into which Jesus came. It was a world where people were misunderstood and slandered, a world where people betrayed trust, a world of violence and bloodshed.

Have you ever heard the saying, "Christmas is for children?" If you are talking about our secular holiday, you may be right. If you're talking about Christmas in the Bible, then Christmas is decidedly not for children. Their ears are, we think, too tender to hear of such things as pregnancy and conception and virginity. Surely we would like to shield them from the sight when Herod's soldiers march down to Bethlehem and kill little babies right and left. Christmas for children? Not at all.

I'll tell you who Christmas is for. Christmas is for people who are coming into adult life and who need to know in advance that it is not going to be all happiness, but that there are going to be shadows along the path. Christmas is for people in mid-life for whom life has lost meaning and they're trying to make some sense out of it. They need direction. They need a pole star to go by. Christmas is for people in later life who need a hope to hang on to when they sometimes have nothing left but hope. Yes, Christmas is for every kind of person you can name *but* children!

In the Bible three things hang together: the innocence of Mary, the divinity of Jesus, and the deliverance of us sinners. Those three things are inseparable. Remove one and you have undermined the others: the innocence of Mary, the divinity of Jesus, the deliverance we need.

So, before the virgin birth of Jesus we all do well to show a bit of humility. We are, after all, continually revising and updating our knowledge. By all that we understand of aerodynamics, the bumblebee cannot fly. But nobody has told the bumblebee of this, so he continues to flit along just the same.

Some years ago a congressman from a western state was bragging about a certain kind of trout he had caught in the waters back home. It happened he was talking to a piscatorial expert. He said, "It's impossible. The kind of fish you describe cannot live in those waters. The temperature's wrong. The current's wrong. Everything's wrong. It's impossible for that species of fish to be in that location." When the congressman went home, he got out his rod and reel, went down to his favorite creek and caught one of them. He put it on ice and shipped it to the expert, who sent back the following telegram: "The science of a lifetime kicked to death by a fact."

When we come to the virgin birth of Jesus, it ought to be easier for people to believe today than ever before. A baby has been born in a test tube. We have now the means to produce a child by a virgin. Now, we still have to have a human father, but if God could create the universe, what problem is it to Him to create one tiny little cell to start the birth process of Jesus? Here is the voice of innocence, "How can these things be?"

Here is the voice of wonder. Every birth occasions in us a feeling of wonder, and every conception. We are told that a cell so tiny you cannot see it swims against the current, breaks through a wall, unites with another cell so tiny you cannot see it. And when the two have joined, they still are so tiny you cannot see them. Then you say, "That's going to be a person six feet tall and 180 pounds." I stand back in wonder and say, "How can these things be?' I know they are, but I express my wonder in the question: "How can these things be?"

That sense of wonder persists. Someday I'm going to ask a physician to thoughtfully consider how he would redesign the human body. Don't you think that would be interesting? I'd like to see what the suggestions might be—leave out the appendix, perhaps. It's interesting to think about. If your nose were not in the location it's in, you could never go out in the rain. If your ears were not where they are, where would you put your eyeglasses? Do you remember Homer and Jethro and the song, "I've got tears in my ears from lying in my bed crying over you?" One verse says, "If you're not careful, you'll percolate yourself to death." If the human body were only slightly rearranged, we might be in a great deal of trouble from an unexpected source. So we wonder at the human body, at the way reproduction allows life to continue. "How can these things be?"

But Mary's sense of wonder was greater than any natural sense of wonder. There are a few interesting words that come up with regard to Mary. One is the word "wonder," the other is the word "ponder." When the angel came, it was wonder. When Jesus was astounding the teachers of the law while but a lad, she went home and pondered these things in her heart. No doubt the wondering and the pondering were with her all her life.

There is a famous sermon by James Stewart entitled, "Our Lost Sense of Wonder." In that sermon he keeps coming back to a little chorus, like the refrain of a song. "Wonder of wonders," he cries, "and every wonder true." We sing about it, "I Stand Amazed in the Presence of Jesus the Nazarene," and "Amazing Grace." We must never lose the sense of wonder in our religion. Someone has said that whenever holy things become commonplace, they cease to be holy.

We wonder that there is forgiveness in a world of vengeance; that love exists in a world of hate. Amidst all the ugliness of sin we still see the beauty of character. These things cause us to wonder. "How can these things be?" Ask it of grace. Ask it of forgiveness. Ask it of love. Ask it of answered prayer. Ask it of the divine presence in our lives. "How can these things be?" I know they are real. I have experienced them, and so have you, but our sense of wonder at them must never cease.

But just for a moment, let's turn that question upside down. If there is a positive sense of wonder at the presence of great virtue, there is also a negative sense of wonder when you see a Christless Christmas. You wonder why anybody bothers. Talk to people about the spirit of Christmas. One person will say, "Oh, you want a donation for the Salvation Army." Somebody else will say, "Oh, you're talking about Dickens' *Christmas Carol*—the spirit of Christmas past, the spirit of Christmas present, and the spirit of Christmas future." For some, all they know about Christmas spirit are the spirits that come in a bottle. We look at all this distortion of Christmas and we cry out, "How can these things be?" How is it possible that our generation has taken the most stunning event of human history and degraded it so? We have robbed it of meaning and left it hollow and empty. "How can these things be?"

If this is the voice of innocence and wonder, it is also the voice of worship. There are five hymns in the opening chapter of the Gospel of Luke. One was written by Mary. We know two things about Mary. We know her character and her mind. She was very bright. In her veins flowed the blood of David; she was a poet like him. Listen to what she said: "He hath scattered the proud in the imagination of their hearts. He hath put down the mighty from their seats ... and the rich he hath sent empty away." Interesting things to say about God, aren't they? Our hymns all talk about the positive things that He has done, but here is a great inspired hymn from Mary that tells us something equally important about God.

And this is a part of Christmas, too. "He scatters the proud. He brings down the rulers. He sends the rich away empty." There is a way in which Christ keeps turning the stream of life and making it run another way. Worship. Christmas leads inevitably to worship. It does so in the Bible. Shepherds, wise men, worship. It does so in our songs: "O come let us adore him, O come let us adore him." Two of our Christmas carols have the identically same chorus, "Come and worship, come and worship." "Joy to the world, the Savior reigns, let men their songs employ." These are all calls to worship.

Christmas, if it does nothing else, points to worship. Always God is being worshiped by someone, somewhere. We ought to put the book of Revelation into our thoughts at Christmas. There are about the throne four and twenty elders and those living creatures who night and day cry, "Holy, holy, holy, Lord God Almighty." *Always* God is worshiped! The question is, "What is the quality of *our* worship?" And do we put *ourselves* among the worshipers? Christmas contributes to the quality of worship. At the heart of that worship is the question, "How can these things be?" We come to the gospel and we discover that the things that cannot be, are. The impossible becomes a reality. Things beyond our imagining have occurred.

Take prayer. If I should tell you to write a letter to the President, for he is sure to read it himself, would you believe it? Would you believe that the eyes of the President would ever see the letter? The odds against that are astronomical! Suppose I tell you to call the President and give him a little advice. Do you think that you can talk to the President on the telephone today?

Is there a person here who does not believe that he could talk to *God* today?

We readily accept the fact that God hears prayer. But if you were told for the very first time that the almighty God of Heaven and earth will listen to what you say, what would be your reaction? "How can these things be?"

If I were to tell you for the very first time that you may be buried with Christ in baptism and resurrected with Christ, you would say, "How can these things be?" Then we come about our little table, eat our little crumb of bread and drink our little sip of wine. You tell me that the eternal Christ is here, and eats and drinks with us. I cry out, "How can these things be?" I do not cry in disbelief, but in worship!

Mary said to the angel, "Be it unto me according to thy word." There's the missing element of worship. Submission. Something needs to happen to make Christmas real in your life. Vachel Lindsay wrote, "Except that Christ be born again tonight in the dreams of all men, saints and sons of shame, the world will never see his kingdom bright, Star of all hearts lead onward through the night." We talk about born-again Christians. Let's talk about a born-again Christ. In a totally different sense of the word, Christ must this season be born again in us.

When our daughter was very young, she said, "Daddy, why do we have Christmas?"

I said, "You know why we have Christmas."

"Oh yes," she said, "It's so Jesus can come."

I think she meant to say, "It's because Jesus has come," but what she said is absolutely accurate. We have Christmas so Jesus can come in us.

O holy Child of Bethlehem,
Descend to us, we pray.
Cast out our sin and enter in,
Be born in us today.
    (Phillips Brooks)

The Clothes of Christ

Ferdinand Hodler, the great Swiss artist, refused to paint the Matterhorn. It was, he said, too great for his canvas. This subject, the clothes of Christ, is too great for any canvas. The text is all of the New Testament, a text too long to read in its entirety. But it is possible to highlight some significant verses that point the way. One might begin with the first reference to the clothes of Christ and compare it with the last reference to the clothes of Christ.

The first is found in Luke.

And she brought forth her firstborn son, and wrapped him in swaddling clothes, and laid him in a manger; because there was no room for them in the inn (Luke 2:7).

The last is found in Revelation 19, beginning at verse 11:

And I saw heaven open, and behold a white horse; and he that sat upon him was called Faithful and True, and in righteousness he doth judge and make war. His eyes were as a flame of fire, and on his head were many crowns; and he had a name written, that no man knew, but he himself. And he was clothed with a vesture dipped in blood: and his name is called The Word of God (Revelation 19:11-13).

See the contrast between His first clothes and His last clothes. When I was young and read that about swaddling clothes, I thought they were something special, something very different and unique. That's not the case. That was the perfectly ordinary garment of the Jewish baby. When a baby was born in that day, they rubbed him in oil. They sprinkled salt on him because of an old tradition. They wrapped strips of cloth like bandages very tightly, binding the legs and arms of the body. They thought that would give strength to the infant. Those were the swaddling clothes. They were perfectly ordinary. To the credit of the shepherds, they were not fooled by that. They still fell down to worship Him, an ordinary-looking baby in ordinary clothes.

This last picture of the clothes of Christ is extraordinary. Here is a vesture dipped in blood, marked with the phrase: "The Word of God." Put them side by side and they teach us two things about Christ. He was so much like us and He was so much unlike us. Those seemingly contradictory ideas are absolutely essential to understanding Jesus. They are the key. If you don't know those two things, you will never understand Him. He was so much like us! He was so much unlike us!

In many fields of knowledge there is a key. Nobody understood early Egyptian history because nobody could read hieroglyphics. Then they found the Rosetta Stone. That stone has the same paragraph written on it three times, in three different languages. One of those languages was well-known. One was Egyptian hieroglyphics. The Rosetta Stone was the key that unlocked our knowledge of ancient Egypt.

Here is the key to understanding Christ. He was so much like us. He had a body like our bodies. He didn't have a body like the Roman god Janus, with two faces, one looking forward and one backward. He didn't have a body like the Hindu god Siva with four arms. He didn't have a body like your second grade teacher who had eyes in the back of her head. He had a body like ours: two eyes, two ears, two arms, two legs. Cut Him and He would bleed. Deny Him rest and He would grow tired. Deny Him water and He would be thirsty. Deny Him food and He would be hungry. Wound Him and He would die. He was so like us. But He was so unlike us. He was tempted as we are tempted, but He never sinned as we sin. He prayed as we pray, but He never *had* to pray the way we *have* to pray. He grew hungry as we grow hungry, but He never made food the essential thing in His life. He worked as we work, but He never made work the central thing in His life. He loved, but He never let it degenerate into lust. Here was one so much unlike us. It's marked by the vesture dipped in blood.

Some say it is the blood of vengeance: the blood of His enemies. That fits the immediate context. He *is* God's avenger, the executor of the wrath of God upon men. We may interpret it that way. But others say it is His own blood, His precious blood, His atoning blood. That fits the larger context of the whole book of Revelation, and that would make this the costliest garment ever worn.

One of the most expensive fabrics in the world is vicuna. It is made from the hair on the throat of certain goats. If you had a dress made out of that, it would cost you thousands and thousands of dollars. Not long ago, they were selling gold lace in London at $151.20 to the yard. These are rags compared to this vesture dipped in blood, His precious blood.

So we learn in His ordinary first clothes and His extraordinary last clothes how much like us He was and how much unlike us He was.

Then let us compare His work clothes and His clothes of wonder. He wore a carpenter's apron. He came to fill the next to the lowest place in the social structure of His day. He did not come as a great spiritual leader might have been expected to come. He did not come as a priest. He did not come as a scribe. He did not come as a great political leader, as a king or governor. He did not come as a great military leader, as a general or a commander. He did not come as a great business leader, a banker or merchant. He did not come even as a schoolteacher, or a physician. He came as a carpenter. The only thing lower than a carpenter was a tanner. Perhaps He would have come as a tanner, except then He would have been barred from the temple where many of His deeds were done. So, He came as a carpenter until He was thirty. Then He donned the robe of a prophet.

Finally, in the upper room, He put on the towel of a servant and washed the disciples' feet. That was the lowest job. The servant who was given the least place in the house was the servant who waited at the door to wash the guests' feet. That's the place He took.

It made headlines in the newspapers and was recorded in the history books that John F. Kennedy said, "Ask not what your country can do for you, but what you can do for your country." The sentiment was expressed far better by Jesus, who said, "I came not to be served, but to serve." "My father works," He said, "and I work."

After the resurrection, Jesus met His disciples by the sea. He fixed their breakfast. The risen, glorified Christ did not think it beneath His dignity to do that. He built a fire. He cleaned the fish. (What a dirty job that is!) He cooked their breakfast. He did not think it beneath Him to do that.

And in His work He showed us the splendor of work, the dignity of work, and the sin of indolence and laziness. The Thracians of ancient Greece thought work was a sin and a shame, so they lived by war. Our Lord thought differently.

There's a book entitled *Dress for Success*. Executives at IBM really believe in that. They require their people to dress in a certain way.

Jesus in His carpenter's apron, Jesus girded with a towel, hardly seem dressed for success. But then once, once, we see Him in robes that befit Him. On the mount of transfiguration He was changed. His garments shone as the light. Those robes of light fit Him perfectly. They fit Him because we associate light with life.

Without light there would be no life on this planet. We associate light with beauty. All of our colors are drawn from a little narrow space on the spectrum of light. We associate light with protection and safety. Now through the laser, we associate light with healing. How appropriate that Christ, who is our life and who gives a new definition to beauty, who is our protector and who is our healer, should be robed in a garment of light.

They say that clothes make the man. Of course, it's not true. Clothes only reveal the man. If you see a teenage boy who has always been careless about his appearance suddenly begin spending an hour at the mirror combing his hair, you know something about him. You know he's found a girl.

You see someone who is very meticulous about his appearance and you know that here is someone who is concerned about detail. You see a person who is careless about his appearance and you know this is someone whose mind is on larger things and gives little thought to details.

We learn a lot about Christ from the clothes that He wears; from His ordinary clothes and His extraordinary clothes, from His work clothes and His clothes of wonder. We learn the most from His dying clothes and His deathless clothes.

There was that scarlet robe they put on Him to mock Him. Where did they get that? That was the uniform of an officer in the Roman army! When they put it on Him, it was at the same time paradoxical and proper. It was paradoxical because He was the Prince of Peace. They meant to mock Him. They put on the Prince of Peace a uniform of war. Yet war and peace are always opposite sides of the same coin. He is the Prince of Peace. He is also the captain of our salvation. He is the Lord of Hosts. His church marches like an army with banners. There *was* a certain appropriateness to what they did when they put the scarlet robe on Him.

Then at the cross they took His seamless robe and gambled for it. That touches us. It was His only possession, and they took it. He didn't own a home. He didn't have any money. He didn't have any land. All that He owned was that one seamless robe, and they took it. Not only was it His only possession; it was a very special possession. It was a seamless robe. That tells us that it was made with special care, by His mother perhaps, or by some friend and supporter who believed in what He was doing. When they took it, they marked indelibly the difference between Him and themselves.

He was one who was always giving, and they were those who were always taking. He had little concern for possessions, and they had concern for little else. He lived by destiny, and they lived by chance. You and I have to choose which will be the pattern for our lives. Will we be givers or takers? Will we be people who have little concern for that which is material or people who have concern for little else? Will we be people who live with a sense of spiritual destiny, or will we be people who live by chance? Having taken His robe, they then crucified the unclothed Christ.

Artists, people of great sensitivity, have always draped the body of Christ on the cross. The fact of the matter is that His executioners stripped Him and nailed Him there! They did it to humiliate Him. They did it to bring Him shame, but they failed. He had an inner dignity they could not touch! Sometimes when I have been going somewhere to speak I have put on my jacket and said, "I've got to put on my dignity." But Christ did not put on His dignity, and they could not take it off. Christ had an inner dignity that they could not take away from Him. They stripped Him of His friends! They stripped Him of His pulpit! They stripped Him of His possessions! They stripped Him of His robe! But they could not strip Him of His dignity!

God saw the unclothed Christ and drew a curtain of darkness over the whole earth. Then after the resurrection and the ascension He put on Him robes so splendid that they are beyond description. Revelation 1:13 says, "dressed in a robe reaching down to his feet and with a golden sash around his chest" *(NIV)*. God clothed Him—clothed Him with power and might and beauty and glory and honor!

Now see the most wonderful thing of all. It's in the chapter with which we began. "There followed him, riding upon white horses, men and women dressed in fine linen, white and clean." Where did they get those robes? You know. He put His robe on them—His robe of righteousness, His robe of purity, His robe of sinlessness. He put His robe on them! He puts His robe on us! Over the rags of our self-righteousness—over the filth of our sin—over the twisted deformity of our broken lives! He puts His robe on us!

I got a robe!
You got a robe!
All God's children got a robe!
When I get to Heaven
Gonna put on my robe!
Gonna walk all over God's Heaven!

His First Miracle

In the second chapter of the Gospel of John this story is told:

On the third day a wedding took place at Cana in Galilee. Jesus' mother was there, and Jesus and his disciples had also been invited to the wedding. When the wine was gone, Jesus' mother said to him, "They have no more wine."

"Dear woman, why do you involve me?" Jesus replied, "My time has not yet come."

"His mother said to the servants, "Do whatever he tells you."

Nearby stood six stone water jars, the kind used by the Jews for ceremonial washing, each holding from twenty to thirty gallons.

Jesus said to the servants, "Fill the jars with water"; so they filled them to the brim.

Then he told them, "Now draw some out and take it to the master of the banquet."

They did so, and the master of the banquet tasted the water that had been turned into wine. He did not realize where it had come from, though the servants who had drawn the water knew. Then he called the bridegroom aside and said,

"Everyone brings out the choice wine first and then the cheaper wine after the guests have had too much to drink; but you have saved the best till now."

This, the first of his miraculous signs, Jesus performed in Cana of Galilee. He thus revealed his glory, and his disciples put their faith in him (John 2:1-11, *NIV*).

Apparently the disciples saw something in this miracle that we don't see. There are three questions that may be asked about it. We can guess that the servants asked, "How did you do that?"

It's interesting that the disciples never asked that of any miracle that Jesus performed. He walked on the water. They never asked, "How did you do that?" He multiplied the loaves and fishes. They never asked, "How did you do that?" They saw the miracles as related to *who* Jesus was, not as related to *how* they were done. They saw the miracles as validating marks of the Christ, answering the question, "Who is He?"

For us there is a third question that surrounds this miracle. That's the question, "Why?" Why did Jesus perform this miracle at all?

I grew up in a culture that believed it was a sin to drink wine. Everybody in our church thought it was a sin to drink wine. Everybody in our town thought it was a sin to drink wine. There was a local law that made it illegal to sell wine in our town. It is still against the law to sell wine in my hometown.

We were really puzzled by this miracle. We wondered why Jesus did it at all. We wondered all the more why it was His first miracle. Surely the first miracle was done by choice and not by chance. Surely Jesus had thought about it in advance. We cannot imagine that He decided on the spur of the moment to perform this miracle. This was his *first* miracle. It must have been chosen deliberately.

We can never really know why Jesus does something. We can't get into His mind or His heart. We can only guess and wonder. But it may be valuable for us to guess and wonder.

We notice this right away. Jesus began His work at a wedding and not at a funeral. A funeral would have been a good choice. A funeral is a solemn occasion. Jesus came to teach us that life has its solemn side. Life is serious business. We are not just here to play and have fun. A solemn occasion like a funeral would have been a good occasion.

Jesus came to fulfill the law. The book of Colossians says that He nailed the law to His cross. The old system was going to die. Thus, a funeral would have been a good place to begin.

Jesus himself came to die. The cross dominates our religion. It is woven into the very fabric of our faith. A funeral would have been a good choice. But Jesus didn't begin His work at a funeral. He began at a wedding.

He began at an occasion of joy, not an occasion of sadness. Joy is the keynote of the New Covenant. When you read the prophets, you don't read much about joy. There are a few such texts. There are not very many. Joy was not a keynote in the message of the prophets. You do find it sometimes in the Psalms, but you find as many tears there as you do notes of joy.

Turn to the New Testament and it is totally different. Many of Jesus' parables dealt with joy. A woman finds a lost coin and says, "Rejoice with me." A man finds a lost sheep and says, "Rejoice with me." A lost boy comes home. His father says, "Let us be merry." A man finds a treasure hidden in a field. He sells everything and buys that field. A man finds a pearl of great price. Jesus told parables about banquets and feasts. More parables are about joy than any other theme.

The apostles picked up that note of joy. "Rejoice in the Lord always," said Paul. "Count it all joy," wrote James. We express it in our worship. We sing, "The joy of the Lord is my strength." We sing, "Joyful, Joyful, We Adore Thee." We sing, "I have the joy, joy, joy, joy down in my heart;" "Rejoice Ye Pure in Heart;" "Joy to the World, the Lord Is Come." These are our songs. So it was appropriate that Jesus should begin His ministry at an occasion of joy, not an occasion of sadness.

We notice, too, that His work began in a small place, not in a large place. It began in a village, not a city. I would have begun in Jerusalem. I would have begun right in front of the temple. I would have performed there some stunning miracle. But Jesus began in Cana, a tiny place. It's not even on a main highway. It's a nowhere place. What a strange place to begin.

But Jesus was not interested in earthly power. He was not

interested in earthly prestige. He was not interested in political influence. He was not interested in pride. He signaled this to us by beginning in this little place.

His interest was in spiritual power, not in any other kind of power. He went to a place where there was no one with influence or power. He went to a village wedding where there were only common people. These were the very people He had come to help.

He had not come to turn kings around. They were beyond help. He had not come to convince the Jewish priests. They were beyond changing. He had come to touch the hearts of the common people. He had come to serve the ordinary man, the ordinary woman. Here there were hearts that were open to Him. Here there were hearts that were tender and would receive Him.

So, He didn't begin in some great city. He didn't begin at some busy street corner. He didn't begin at some great crossroads of commerce. He began in this little out-of-the-way place—Cana.

He began at a minor occasion, not a major occasion. I have performed many weddings. To me it is quite routine. For the couple getting married it is never routine. They make elaborate plans. They make elaborate preparations. Everything must be just right. They are very nervous. But for me it's just part of a day's work. It's a minor event.

It was so with the village wedding in Cana. It was a major event to the families involved, of course. But in the great scheme of world affairs what is one village wedding?

Jesus had so many other opportunities. The Jews had great feast days and holy days. Why not begin on one of them? Why not begin at the feast of the Passover? Or the feast of Tabernacles? Why not begin at Pentecost? There were many great national holidays. Why begin with a simple wedding? The answer may be this: Jesus was not interested in earthly kingdoms.

Too soon He had a problem with that. Too soon they wanted to make Him an earthly king. Sometimes He had to withdraw from a crowd or go to another place because they wanted to make Him a king. The disciples thought of Him as an earthly king. In the beginning they saw Him as a national deliverer. So, He chose to pass over the great days on the calendar of His people. He chose this simple event. It was an important event to that family. Jesus had a role to play in families.

I read about a senator. Someone wrote him a letter. He was asked to intervene on behalf of an individual who had a problem. He replied that he was so busy working for the nation that he had no time for individuals! Jesus didn't come just to help the nation. He came to do something for every little family. He wanted to get into every home. He wanted to be a part of every family. He still does. He signaled it by beginning His work at a wedding.

More than that, He came to make us a family. That's our relationship to Him. That's our relationship to one another. It's a relationship of family. It's more intimate than any other relationship. By beginning at a wedding Jesus showed us that we are the family of God. He wanted to show us that He was concerned about little things. He didn't limit himself to the great issues of world affairs. He was also concerned about little things.

I think it is safe to say that anything that worries you concerns Him. Whatever troubles you troubles Him. We teach our little children to pray. The concerns they bring to the Lord are very small. They are little, childish things. But we believe that He hears those prayers. We believe they are important to Him.

Try to imagine the scene when the children came to Jesus. We know what He did. He blessed them. What do you think they did? What do you think they said to Him? What little concerns did they come to tell Him about? Whatever they were, don't you think He listened?

There's something more about this first miracle. It was symbolic, not practical. We must say that it certainly was not practical. What difference would it make if they ran out of wine at the wedding? At the worst, the host would be embarrassed. Jesus didn't come to save us from embarrassment. That is surely not a major concern of His. So, we must say that it was symbolic, not practical.

Let me tell you how I would have begun. I think my first miracle would have been to raise someone from the dead. Now that would get people's attention! What a way to begin! That's what I would have done. But when Jesus did raise somebody from the dead, they tried to kill Jesus. Not only that, they tried to kill the man He raised from the dead. Maybe my idea is not such a good one.

Perhaps then I might begin with some act of healing. Perhaps I'd heal some leper or give sight to some blind person. That would be a good beginning. But then that's more private than public. It affects only one person. Maybe that's not a good choice.

What about feeding the five thousand? What a miracle that was! But if one began with that, then people would expect to receive bread and fish every day. People would remember the manna in the wilderness and quickly volunteer, "Count me in," they'd say. I guess that's not a good choice either. All of my choices have their problems. So, I've come back to Jesus' choice.

Can we guess why Jesus chose this miracle as the first miracle? I am convinced that it is symbolic. It is symbolic in two ways. There are three things about water. It has no taste. It has no color. It has no nutritional value. There are three things about wine. It has taste. It has color. It has some nutritional value.

I believe this miracle is a parable. It's a parable of the things Jesus intended to do for us. He does to our lives what he did to that water. Without Christ our lives are colorless, tasteless, and have little real value. When Christ comes into our lives they are changed. Our lives have color and taste. Our lives have value in the world. Jesus changes our lives dramatically! It's as dramatic as that first miracle so long ago. What were we before Christ came into our lives? What would we be today without Him? The miracle may be a parable, acted rather than spoken.

It's also symbolic in at least one other way. Jesus came to this world to perform a wedding. He came to this world to unite man and God. Sin had separated us. It seemed there was nothing that could bring us together. God was so holy. We were so sinful. How could we possibly be brought together? That was the task Jesus faced. That was the task Jesus performed. He united us to God. He came to perform a wedding. The striking thing is this: the ministry of Jesus that began with a wedding ends with a wedding. You can read about it in the book of Revelation. It's not in a village but in a city. It's not on earth but in Heaven. It doesn't create a union that will last only until death separates. It unites forever. The first miracle of Jesus must be placed alongside the last chapters in the Bible. In a sense, the gospel begins and ends with a wedding. There may be far more to that than we will ever know or understand.

Listen to the description of that last great wedding:

Then I heard what sounded like a great multitude, like the roar of rushing waters and like loud peals of thunder, shouting:

"Hallelujah!

For our Lord God Almighty reigns.

Let us rejoice and be glad and give him glory!

For the wedding of the Lamb has come,

and his bride has made herself ready . . ."

Then the angel said to me, "Write: Blessed are those who are invited to the wedding supper of the Lamb!"

(Revelation 19:6, 7, 9, NIV)

His Last Miracle

Jesus' knees are still damp with the dew of Gethsemane's garden. He has knelt in agony and prayer while the disciples slept. Now He awakens them. The full moon bathes the Judean hills in its light, but underneath the olive trees it is dark. In the distance the lights of torches may be seen, coming down from Jerusalem, across the Kidron Valley. Several men arrive at the garden. Jesus meets them at the gate.

"Whom are you seeking?" He asks.

"Jesus of Nazareth," they answer.

"I am He." They fall back into the shadows.

The question is repeated, and the answer.

Then a familiar figure steps out of the shadows. It is Judas! He plants a kiss on Jesus' cheek! The officers move in to make their arrest! A sword flashes in the moonlight! Our text describes that dramatic moment!

And one of them smote the servant of the high priest, and cut off his right ear. And Jesus answered and said, Suffer ye thus far. And he touched his ear and healed him. (Luke 22:50, 51)

I call it His last miracle. It was not, of course. It was followed by that miracle of miracles, the resurrection. And that was followed by the continuing miracles of the church and of conversion. But it was the last miracle of His ministry; the last miracle of healing His hands performed. And that last miracle is a microcosm of His ministry. It is His whole ministry in miniature. It is as if every sermon He preached, every sign He performed, every parable He told were all gathered together, distilled and the essence of them reproduced in this single dramatic event.

Here We See His Control of All Situations

Who is in charge here? Not Judas! He darts in to plant his venomous kiss and disappears. Not the officers! They shrink in the shadows until Jesus bids them do their duty. Jesus is in charge here! He has the power to halt the proceedings at any point. It was the same power seen when He cleansed the temple and drove its merchants before Him like leaves before the autumn wind. It was the same power that held back the murderous crowd at Nazareth that wanted to throw him over a cliff. It was the same power that stopped the officers who, sent to arrest Jesus, were themselves arrested by His words.

Here is power to heal. What must have raced through Malchus' mind when Jesus raised His hand! Will He slap me? Will He choke me? Will He strike me dead? But that hand had never been lifted in vengeance against any man. And it never would be.

It is often true that power corrupts. How else shall we explain the Caesars and the dictators of history? How else can we account for the petty politicians and the small town tyrants? But power does not always corrupt. It did not corrupt Jesus. Christians must not shrink from their duty as citizens. Power need not corrupt.

Jesus' power was always controlled. We sing of "gentle Jesus, meek and mild," but our understanding of gentleness and meekness is sometimes inaccurate. Meek does not mean weak. Meek does not say "I can't." Meek says "I won't." Jesus could have called twelve legions of angels. He called none.

Some say that Michelangelo's greatest masterpiece is his statue of Moses. He has carved Moses larger than life. The muscles ripple across the marble. It is a sculpture of unmistakable strength and power. Beneath it Michelangelo wrote a line from Deuteronomy: "Moses, the Meek."

Here We See His Compassion for All People

I would never have healed Malchus. I would have thought his missing ear an appropriate souvenir of that awful night of infamy. And if I had healed him I think I would have put the ear on upside down!

Suppose Jesus had not healed him. Human nature has not changed much. Whenever you meet a person without an arm, or hand, or finger, you sooner or later ask, "How did it happen?" Everyone who met Malchus would have finally gotten around to the question, "What happened to your ear?" And Malchus would have had to answer, "A Christian did that!"

Jesus healed him and taught us compassion for an enemy. He not only told us to love our enemies—He did it! He did it on the cross! He did it at the judgment! He did it here in the garden. Jesus' first miracle was for a stranger and His last miracle was for an enemy. Not only so, but His last recorded prayer was a prayer for His enemies.

We see also His compassion for a friend. He does not say to Simon Peter, "Can't you do anything right? You almost missed him altogether!" Nor did He say, "Simon, you dummy. For three years I've been telling you I must go to the cross. I have told you my kingdom is not of this world. Can't you understand anything?" No, Jesus simply said, "Suffer ye thus far," and healed him. Thus He taught us how to forgive our friends. That may be a good deal harder than forgiving our enemies. After all, we don't expect much from our enemies. We expect a great deal from our friends. When they disappoint us, it is very difficult to accept it. We forget how often we may have disappointed them. We forget how often all of us may disappoint God!

Later, we see Jesus' compassion for His family as He commits Mary to the care of John. Perhaps we are here most lacking in compassion. If we treated our friends as politely as strangers, if we treated the members of our household as considerately as the guests in our home, how different life would be. The people we love the best we sometimes treat the worst. If forgiving an enemy is difficult, and if forgiving a friend is harder still, to forgive your family is hardest of all. But that is a compassion we must learn.

We see reflected here His compassion for all men. He had time for Nicodemus, that self-righteous know-it-all. He had time for the woman at the well, a Samaritan and an adulteress. He had time for cowardly Pilate. He had time for Zacchaeus, that little man whose heart was even smaller than his stature. We would have passed every one of them by. He passed none of them by.

We never *need* to sing, "Pass me not, O gentle Savior; Do not pass me by." The danger is not that He will pass us by, but that we will pass Him by. I like to think of the song as more of a confession than a petition, as sung more for our benefit than His.

Here We See His Composure at All Times

With what poise and serenity Jesus went about His ministry. With what frustration I go about mine! He was not annoyed by the pressure of the crowds. He was not surprised by the power of the demons. He was not baffled by the questions of the Pharisees. He was not frustrated be the quarrels of the twelve. He could face the need of a hungry multitude, the threat of a storm on the sea, or the thievery of the temple merchants without ever losing His composure.

He was in command of every situation. How did He manage it? Because He was always in command of himself. "He that rules this spirit [is better than] he that takes a city," says the book of Proverbs. I would like to think that I, too, could keep my composure in every situation. I would like to think that no matter what my doctor told me, or my lawyer told me, or my accountant told me, or my friends told me, or my family told me, that I could remain composed and serene.

How is it possible? Jesus was in command of every situation because He was always in command of himself. And I can be in command of every situation, if I will let Him be in command of my life.

I wonder if Malchus ever thought about that right ear. I wonder if he looked in the mirror and mused about that fateful night. I wonder if his ear smarted more from the touch of Jesus than it had stung from the sword of Simon. I wonder if he ever said, "This right ear is not really mine. It belongs to Christ. He gave it to me."

What about that blind man at Jericho, to whom Jesus gave sight. Do you think he ever said, "These are not my eyes. They belong to Christ. He gave them to me"?

What about that deaf stammerer whom Jesus healed. Do you think he ever said, "This is not my voice. It belongs to Christ. He gave it to me"?

What about that lame man whom Jesus made whole. Do you think he ever said, "These are not my legs. They belong to Christ. He gave them to me"?

What about you? Have you ever said, "These are not my hands, my feet, my ears, my eyes. This is not my mind. This is not my life. They all belong to Christ. He gave them to me"?

General William Booth was the founder of the Salvation Army. Toward the end of his career, he was interviewed by the press. As he looked back over his lifetime, this is what he said: "God had all there was of me. There have been others who had greater plans and greater opportunities than I; but from the day I had a vision of what God could do, I made up my mind that God would have all there was of William Booth."

Does God have *all there is* of you?

The Importance of Nicknames

A great many had come out for spring training, but now the season was about to begin and it was time for the coach to make the cut. He called them all together and from the group selected those few whose names would actually appear on the roster. That is precisely what happened in Mark 3:13-19.

Some surprising names are on this list. Everybody is surprised to see Judas Iscariot here. There are many explanations for Jesus choosing Judas. The one I like best is that Judas had a potential that could have run either way. He could have become a famous apostle. He became an infamous traitor. Is it not possible that the world's worst gangster had also the potential to have become a saint instead? Is it not true that the world's great saints could have chosen instead to be criminals? Potential for greatness is capable of cutting either way. After Jesus chose Judas, Judas chose which path he would take. If you have great talent, or energy, remember that it offers for you two potentials—one inspiring and one frightening.

More surprising than the name of Judas is to find here Matthew and Simon the Canaanite. When Judas was chosen nobody thought he would turn out to be a traitor. When Matthew was chosen everybody thought he was already a traitor. Matthew was a publican, a tax collector for the Roman government. He was a collaborator with the enemy.

During World War II, a Norwegian military officer made a secret trip to see Hitler. Shortly after, Hitler invaded Norway, met half-hearted resistance, and set up a puppet government. He put that officer at its head. His name was Quisling. That name so stood for betrayal that it entered the language and you can find it today in the dictionary as a synonym for traitor. Matthew was regarded as a quisling.

At the opposite end of the political spectrum was Simon the Canaanite, whom Luke calls the Zealot. The Zealots were a political party who wanted to arm the people and mount a rebellion against Rome. Simon was as far to the right as Matthew was to the left. They were as far apart as a Communist and a fascist, yet Jesus thought He could use both of them—on the same team!

Let's be sure that ours is a church you can belong to no matter your political affiliation. Some churches today would not welcome you if you hold certain political views! Whatever your politics, you can be a Christian.

In Judas and Matthew and Simon we learn that Jesus saw the potential in people that others could not see. James, the son of Alphaeus, is a good example. The Bible calls him James the Less, not because he was less important than that other James, the brother of John. He was called James the Less because he was short of stature. "Little Jim," Jesus called him, or "Shorty."

Can't you picture someone saying, "But he doesn't look like an apostle!" Some surely thought an apostle must have a commanding and striking appearance. That's important to presidential candidates. King Saul's early success lay in the fact that he looked like a king. As it turned out, looks were deceiving. Jesus saw in James, Judas, Simon, and Matthew the potential that others could not see.

Not only are there surprising names on the list. Jesus surprisingly changed three of their names, giving them nicknames.

Nicknames are interesting. Sometimes they are given because they do not fit. A large person will sometimes be called "Tiny." Most often, they are given because they do fit.

Jesus called Simon "Peter," which means "rock." He did not

seem much like a rock. He was changeable and undependable. But Jesus knew what he was going to become. Some of our hardest rocks were once liquid. Granite was once molten, but it hardened into a very strong substance. So did Simon Peter. When Jesus gave him that nickname it shows that Jesus saw the potential in him that others could not see.

James and John, the sons of Zebedee, He nicknamed the "Sons of Thunder." If He had called them "Lightning" it would have been easy to understand. They wanted to call down fire from Heaven on an unbelieving village that rejected Christ. Lightning kills. Thunder never kills; it only warns.

But Jesus saw what lay ahead. He knew that this James would be the first of the twelve to lay down his life for Him. That death would be a warning of worse persecution to come. The other of the Sons of Thunder, John, would be the last of the twelve to die. Before he died, he would write the greatest book of warning in the New Testament, the book of Revelation. Yes, in these two brothers Jesus saw the potential that others missed.

In us He sees the potential that others miss. I suppose colleges have quit selecting the boy and girl most likely to succeed. They were fooled too often. It would be interesting to know the potential your parents saw in you, the potential your friends see in you, the potential you see in yourself. What an interesting comparison that would make. Christ sees great spiritual potential in you. Will you try to be aware of that? And sensitive to that?

A column of marble lay for fifty years in the workyard of the cathedral at Florence. It had been poorly blocked at the quarry. More than that, the sculptor Duccio had started to use it, made a deep cut in the middle, and abandoned it. Over those fifty years, many sculptors came by to measure that piece of stone, but all said it was useless. The gouge ran too deep. But when Michelangelo measured that stone he saw in it a potential that others missed. He saw imprisoned in that stone a David. Today that statue of David is regarded as the most beautiful on earth. From all over the world men and women come to Florence to see it. Michelangelo saw in the rejected stone the potential others missed.

In the early days of the Civil War when things were going badly for the Union, President Lincoln wrote to General McClel-

Ian: "If you are not planning to do anything with the Army, will you lend it to me for a while?" God is saying to you, "If you are not planning to do anything with your life, will you lend it to me for a while?" *NOT PETER but HIS CONFESSION*

Christ did more than see the hidden potential in men. He helped them realize that potential. By calling Simon a "rock" He helped him to become more dependable. He tried more and more to live up to the name Jesus had given him. When James and John were called the Sons of Thunder, it had a subtle but certain effect on their lives. We all tend to be like the image we think others have of us. We live up to that image—or we live down to it.

Call the prettiest girl ugly, do it often enough and convincingly enough, and she will become ugly. Her mouth will drop and twist, her brow will wrinkle, and it will become a self-fulfilling prophecy. Take a bright child, convince him he is stupid, and he will be. Jesus knew that. That's why He gave nicknames to some of the twelve.

Even in the Old Testament you find God changing men's names. Abram He called "Abraham," which means "father of many nations." A man conducts himself differently when he believes that that is his destiny! God changed Jacob's name to Israel. The "el" in Israel is the name of God. He gave Jacob His own name. A person conducts himself differently when he wears the name of his God. Isn't that part of what is behind our name, Christian? Did not Christ want us to be conscious of our vocation as the Christlike ones?

If you were a Rockefeller or a Roosevelt, would there be a kind of obligation to live up to such a name? Wouldn't it put a certain responsibility on you? But ours is a higher obligation. We wear the name of Christ!

If a man has gained a reputation for expertise in some field, he works to keep it. I am not a poet. I can compose any kind of doggerel and put it out. A poet who has a reputation cannot do that. He has to be careful what goes out under his name. A great composer can't just sit down at the piano and play *Chopsticks*.

As Christians we have a reputation to uphold. We can't get out of it by refusing the name. It is a name the Lord gives us. None of us decided to name ourselves Christian. Peter didn't say,

"Lord, I hate my name. Call me Rocky." No, the Lord changed his name and the Lord changed yours. When He did He put you under obligation to try to live up to it.

We need also to see that Christ used them as they were. Even before any of these twelve had reached their potential Christ used them. While they were becoming what they could be He used them. He did not wait until they were mature.

In the Southwest, the Indians used to eat the yucca plant. I have eaten yucca, and I know how it got its name. The interesting thing is that they ate all parts of the plant. They ate the bud. They ate the flower. They ate the fruit. So God uses us in all stages of our development.

That has so impressed some people that they have misapplied a passage of Scripture. How many times we hear quoted, "A little child shall lead them." Unfortunately, that is not the meaning of that passage. But we all have seen children and young people used of God. Indeed, through every stage of life God has some work for you to do. Even when you are old and your energies are spent, God will use you in some way.

In Ephesians 4, Paul speaks of various fields of service and adds, "till we all come . . . unto a perfect man, unto the measure of the stature of the fulness of Christ." That won't happen until we get to Heaven. But while we are growing spiritually, while we are maturing spiritually, even then He wants us to serve Him.

Nobody would have guessed that God could use the woman at Jacob's well. Women did not have a public role in that day. And she was a sinful woman, an ostracized woman. Yet she met Christ and then ran into the village to lead others to Him. Nobody would have picked her for an evangelist. Yet she led more people to Christ during the days of His flesh than any other person recorded in the Bible. Perhaps nobody has picked you for greatness—except God.

That call to service is so often ignored, and so often put off. Our Christianity is too often like Averell Harriman's French. Harriman once said, "My French is excellent, all except the verbs." Our Christianity may be lacking in verbs!

John Greenleaf Whittier was thinking of unrequited love

rote: "For of all sad words of tongue or pen, The
~e these—'It might have been.'" But sadder than unre-
~ve is unfilled potential. Thomas Gray wrote of that in
gy Written in a Country Churchyard:

Full many a gem of purest ray serene
The dark unfathomed caves of ocean bear;
Full many a flower is born to blush unseen,
And waste its sweetness on the desert air.

Everyone has a vivid picture of some life of unfulfilled potential. For me, the picture is of a church custodian I once knew. He
started out to be a concert organist, but lacked the money to go
on. So he took a job as a letter carrier for the post office. Then he
retired and took a job as church custodian. But he'd stop in his
duties to play the organ. He wore a gambler's green eye shade to
protect his eyes from the glare. He'd sit there in a dark and
empty church, in his coveralls and his green eye shade and play
Bach, flawlessly, on the church organ. Hearing him, one
thought of Whittier's line: "It might have been. It might have
been."

Saddest of all is to see the unfilled spiritual potential of life.
We think of the unfulfilled potential of Judas, Diotrephes, King
Saul, and a dozen others.

Harold Bell Wright, the novelist, said that he always kept
before him a picture of Christ. He said that he wrote the best
chapters in his books while looking into the face of the Son of
God. So do we write the best chapters in the book of life when
we are "looking unto Jesus."

Visitors to Haiti usually try to see the massive citadel built by
King Henri Christopher almost 200 years ago. On a mountain-
top high above the Carribbean stands this massive fort. Twenty
thousand men died carrying up the stones to build it and the
cannons to defend it. But the invasion never came, no shot was
ever fired. That citadel has stood there for two centuries and
never been used.

Is that going to be the story of your life?

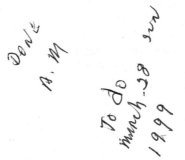

Faith for the Storm

God works in mysterious ways,
His wonders to perform.
He plants his footsteps on the sea
And rides upon the storm.

That little poem has seemed so true that it has often been mistaken for Scripture. It's not Scripture, but it certainly spotlights Mark 6:45-51.

The Sea of Galilee is below the level of the Mediterranean Sea and subtropical in climate. A very short distance away towers Mt. Hermon. The cold air falls on the Sea of Galilee and from the sea the warm moist air rises. When the two clash, you know what is going to happen. Those storms come suddenly and fiercely on the Sea of Galilee. In that sea are twelve men in a little boat. Four of them have lived all their lives in Galilee and have made their living off that sea. They know it well. They know it enough to respect it. They have seen what it can do.

At a church conference on Prince Edward Island in Canada they asked a layman from one of the island's churches to sing a solo. He'd lived all his life in the Maritimes. He'd made his living as a lobsterman. Often he had challenged the sea in his

81

boat. It seemed marvelously appropriate that he
er, the Tempest is Raging."

night they toiled in the sea until in the fourth watch
ne to them. Now, this is an actual event that occurred at
a ve definite time and place in human history. Yet through all
the ages Christians have seen this event as a kind of parable of
human life. It's reflected in a once popular song, "Into Each Life
Some Rain Must Fall." If the rain falls, the winds must come and
the storms. They are inevitable, are they not? The storms of life!
There is no way that we can escape them. Sooner or later the
ship of our life must weather a storm much like this storm.

There are some who think that if you are always a good person and always behave yourself, you will never have to go
through stormy seas. But how did the disciples find themselves
in this situation? Was it because of their disobedience? No, it
was quite the opposite. It was because they obeyed the Lord. If
they had disobeyed Him and stayed on the shore, they would
have been safe. Nor were they out there on some foolish errand
of their own. If that had been the case, we could have easily
understood it. But they were there because Jesus commanded
them to be there. He told them to get into the ship and go to the
other side.

Those who obey the Lord and follow His will are going to sail
through rough seas. Never suppose that if you are a good Christian you will always have sunny days and smooth sailing. The
storms of life are inevitable. They come upon the good and the
bad. As the rain falls on the just and the unjust, so the wind
blows on the evil and good.

In His parable of the builder, Jesus never suggested that the
person who built his house on the rock would not find storms
attacking that house, but rather that the house would withstand
the storm. That's the difference. In the book of Job, you find
God accused of sparing the righteous from the storms of life.
But you read further in the book and discover that that was just
another of the devil's lies. It does a lot of good to be a Christian,
but one thing it does not do is spare you life's storms.

What are the storms of life through which we pass? They may
differ with each individual. There are storms of illness when we
wonder if these bodies are going to last us as long as they ought.

82

There are storms of disappointment. We have life all worked out and then someone comes along and kicks over our tower of blocks. Sometimes guilt is the storm of life through which we must sail. Sometimes it is sorrow. There are many different experiences in life which may fit this picture of a stormy sea and there are many different reactions to these storms.

It's interesting that the same wind capsizes some ships and drives others into a safe harbor. Have you ever wondered about that? After a tornado or a hurricane some people will go to church who haven't gone to church in years. But other people in that community will say, "If this is the way God is going to treat me, I'll have nothing more to do with Him." Why does tragedy drive some people from God and some people to God?

Cleaning up the debris on my lawn after a storm, I got the answer. I noticed that the wind blew only the dead limbs off the trees. That's the answer! The storm will blow away the dead limbs but not the ones that have a living connection to the tree. Jesus said, "I am the vine, you are the branches." If you are connected to the vine, the wind may toss you about but it will not destroy you. If that connection to the vine is interrupted and you become a dead branch, sooner or later the winds of life will blow you away.

There is, however, one unvarying reaction to the storms of life. Fear! Like the disciples we are sometimes afraid. We are afraid more often than we are willing to admit, and more often than we ourselves recognize. Fear disguises itself in many different ways. But whether it is illness or sorrow or disappointment or discouragement or failure or guilt, sooner or later we find ourselves in the same boat with the disciples. We are afraid, and then Jesus comes to us as He came to them. That's the beauty of this story—not the sudden storm, but the surprising appearance of the Savior.

The storms of life are well known and common to human experience. How are we to get through them? What help is there for us? We must turn our eyes to the Savior. Notice at what time He comes to them. It is not at once. They toil through the night, then He comes. He comes when their strength is gone. He comes when their hope is gone. In the fourth watch of the night, while it is yet dark, He comes. "Just when I need him, Jesus is near, Just when I falter, just when I fear." And the chorus says, "Just when I need him most."

Isn't that the lesson here? Isn't that the very heart of this story? Just when I need Him most, He comes to me. In the dark of night, He comes. Notice also that He did not remove them from their situation. He came to share their situation.

Jesus had the power to reach down, pick up that little boat and set it on the mountain where it would be safe. He said that faith could remove mountains. Couldn't it remove boats, too? Or could not Jesus have reached down and rescued them one by one, as a modern-day helicopter extends its rope to pluck men from the sea?

Surely He could have done that, but He did not remove them from their situation. He came to them in their situation. The application of that to life is obvious, isn't it? We keep praying, "Lord, get me out of this," and instead of getting us out of it, He comes and joins us in the middle of it. He shares our situation.

If there is any important lesson to learn in the gospel, it is this: *He shares our situation. He comes to share our fears. He comes to share our disappointments. He comes to share our pain.* He may not take us out of that situation. But the fact that He is there with us makes a difference. If you've had the pleasure of His company, you know it makes a difference. We do not sail alone through life.

He came after their energies were spent. They rowed all night. They tried to get to shore by theirs own power and failed. Then He came and said, "Try my power." The winds were contrary. If you have ever tried to row into the wind, you know what a difficult and tiring thing it is. It is possible to make progress when the winds are contrary, but not by rowing. You hoist a sail. Even if the wind is blowing from the wrong direction you can get where you want to go.

But they did not hoist a sail and claim that divine power to reach their destination. They just kept rowing away by human muscle power and they got nowhere. Have we sometimes done that? Have we sometimes said to God, "I want to do it myself?" Have not our pride and ego caused us to try to accomplish the spiritual victories of life in our own human power and strength? And we have failed, over and over and over again. It's time to hoist the sail of the soul and catch the wind of the Spirit.

So many Scriptures fit beautifully into this theme. Jesus likened the Holy Spirit to the wind; the powerful wind that moves ships and turns windmills and generators. "That's what the Holy Spirit is like," Jesus said to Nicodemus. And as these toilers upon the sea could have harnessed the wind to their advantage so you and I can allow the Holy Spirit to empower our lives. We don't have to do it ourselves. Indeed we cannot do it ourselves. The wind of the Spirit can do it through us.

So the apostle Paul said, "It is no longer I that live, it is Christ that lives in me." Paul could not live life successfully. Christ in Paul could live successfully. "I can do all things," he said, "through Christ which strengtheneth me." What he meant was "Christ can do all things through me."

Notice, too, that He came on the sea. Did He not have more than one alternative? Couldn't He have come in some other fashion? *The very thing that threatened them supported Him.* He came upon the very thing they feared. Mark that lesson down in life. How many times has Christ come to men through illness? How many times has Christ walked on the waves of disappointment to come into our lives? How many times have the storms of guilt swept over us and then Jesus has come to us? There is a purpose in tragedy. Now, I do not believe that Jesus sent this storm on the Sea of Galilee. It came by natural, physical, meteorological reasons that are clearly understandable to any weatherman. But once the storm had come, Jesus made it the road over which He traveled.

Never has it been the case that our Lord has made you sick. Never has it been the case that He has defeated you or frustrated you or disappointed you. But when those things happen, He comes upon them. He makes them the highway over which He travels. "He rides upon the storm."

I gave a little quiz to a group of very good Bible students. I listed a number of quotations that are supposed to come from the Bible. One of them was that very verse, "God works in mysterious ways, his wonders to perform. He plants his footsteps on the sea and rides upon the storm." A decided majority checked that that was in the Bible. One stayed and argued with me for twenty minutes, assuring me that as soon as she got home she was going to look it up and call me and give me the reference. Why are people so absolutely sure that that's in the Bible? Experience has taught them that it's true! He rides upon the storm! The verse is not in the Bible, but the lesson is.

Notice also the difference between his reaction and theirs. How frightened they are. How calm he is. I wish I could go through life like that, don't you? – serene, poised, calm, and without fear. I'd like to live like that, wouldn't you? You can! He can give you that serenity, that calmness. He'll come into your life as He came onto the ship. He'll say, "Peace, be still." You'll know a peace you can't describe.

Again and again across the years, men and women have heard the words of Jesus as they were spoken on that stormy night so long ago, "Be of good cheer, it is I, be not afraid."

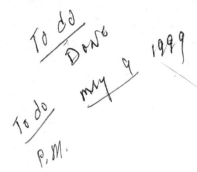

My Father's House

No word came more easily to the lips of Jesus than the word, "Father." He spoke of God as His Father in a way so natural it almost surprises us. He did it so often that He changed the very vocabulary of faith. Ever since, believers have not hesitated to pray as Jesus prayed, "Our Father."

Among the texts in which Jesus used the expression, "My Father," none is more impressive than this, and none is more familiar. It's in John, chapter 14:

Let not your heart be troubled; ye believe in God, believe also in me. In my Father's house are many mansions: if it were not so, I would have told you. I go to prepare a place for you. And if I go and prepare a place for you, I will come again, and receive you unto myself; that where I am, there ye may be also (John 14:1-3).

In this text is a useful strategy for life. "Let not your heart be troubled." Jesus assumes we can control the things we think about. We often say that we cannot. We say that thoughts come to us unbidden and there is nothing we can do about them. But it's evident at the very beginning of this Scripture passage that

Jesus intended for us to control our thoughts. We do not have to concentrate on all the ugly, miserable, mean things of life. We can also open our eyes to the beautiful, glorious, and encouraging things of life.

Some people completely concentrate on the dark side of life. They fix their minds on it and see nothing else. If there were a rainbow about their heads, they wouldn't see it. Once a bloodhound is put on a certain scent, he stays on it regardless of any other scents that may come his way. Once a heat-seeking missile is programmed for a certain target, it goes to that target no matter what happens. People sometimes think like that. They are programmed and their target is the miserable, the mean, and the ugly. That's what they think about. That's all they think about. Showers of blessings may come down upon them, but all they see are the dark clouds and all they hear is the thunder.

Jesus tells us, "Learn how to control your thoughts." There is something more powerful than the mind, and that is the spirit. The spirit can control the mind. We need to learn to control our thoughts and to think good thoughts even in the midst of life's unhappy moments. Jesus did. He went through a life of incredible activity, under constant pressure, and yet was serene and calm. No businessman, no professional man, is under half the pressure that Jesus was. No mother, no housewife is under half the pressure Jesus was. Beside the ordinary pressures of His life, there stood before Him always the shadow of that cross. He knew when and where and how He must die. That burden must have been the heaviest of all. Yet Jesus went around saying, "Be of good cheer" and "My peace I give to you." He had learned to direct His thoughts to the good and wholesome things of life and not to concentrate on the things that were depressing.

Look at the apostle Paul. What a terribly difficult life he lived! He was constantly in danger. His life was in jeopardy every day. He said, "I die daily." That meant he was always threatened by death. Yet he wrote, "Rejoice in the Lord, always. And again I say, rejoice." Here is a strategy for life. Let's not let the world about us control our thoughts. Let's not let events control our thoughts. Let's not let others control our thoughts. Let's take control. "Let not your heart be troubled."

There is also in this text a vivid memory, "my Father's house."

Is it going too far to suppose that when Jesus spoke of the Father's house there was in His mind a memory of a certain house on a certain street in which He once had lived? My wife grew up in a parsonage, the daughter of a minister. Then she married a minister and lived in a series of parsonages. Later when she took a class at university, she wrote a paper about all those parsonages she had lived in. She called it "My Father's House." You can see the double meaning in it. She wrote about the little cramped house she'd lived in with her parents, and then about that too large house in which their furniture seemed lost, a house so large nobody could keep it warm. She wrote about a house she'd lived in with me. It had a coal furnace in the basement which sometimes belched enormous black clouds up through the house, a parsonage we laughingly christened "On Top of Old Smokey." She wrote of that other house we not so humorously named "The Pigeon Roost." To speak of the father's house brought to her mind certain vivid memories of earthly houses in which she'd lived. Was it not so with Jesus?

Could Jesus, speaking of the Father's house, not be at least to some degree thinking of a house in Nazareth filled with precious memories? I want to describe that house for you. No one can visit that house. You can go to the house where George Washington lived. You can go to the house where Abraham Lincoln was born. But no one can go to the house where Jesus lived. It disappeared long ago. But we know what it was like. We know what life was like in the village of Nazareth. We know what the life of a carpenter was like in Jesus' day. We have a fairly accurate idea of the kind of house in which Jesus grew up.

The house was on a narrow unpaved dirt street. It was right up against the street at the front. It was made of mud plastered onto a framework of reeds. It had one tiny window. It had one door and that door led into one single room. It had a dirt floor. Over in the corner were the bedrolls, rolled out onto the floor at night to make a pallet and rolled up and stored in the corner by day. There were few items of furniture. There was a lampstand. Do you remember Jesus' illustration of a lampstand? It was a little shelf that held a stone lamp. There was a basket or tub that held flour. When it was empty it could be turned upside down to make a table. Then the lamp could be set on top of it, but never under it, of course. There was a hand mill made of two round stones. Here the grain was ground. Because Joseph was a carpenter there probably was also a wooden stool or two, and maybe a table. Outside there was a stairway that led to the roof. The rooftop served as a second room. There was a rude shelter on the roof. Here the grain and the flax dried. Here was a small pile of firewood. That was the kind of house in which Jesus grew up. That was the kind of house in which He lived until He was thirty. With that picture in mind it is amazing to think of Jesus speaking of "my Father's house."

Perhaps there was in Jesus' mind a more vivid memory, not of a house in Nazareth, but of a home in Nazareth. It was a place where people felt accepted; where people knew they were loved; where there was security. It was a place where you could sense the firmness, the dependability, the consistency. Jesus must surely have grown up in such a home. Surely God chose well when He chose Mary to be the mother of our Lord.

We catch a glimpse into the home life of Jesus when we read about His mother and His brothers coming to try to persuade Him to abandon His ministry and come back home. They knew He was working too hard. They knew He had opposition. They wanted to spare Him and they urged Him to come home. This was a home where He was welcome, where He was loved, where somebody cared about Him. This memory must surely have been fresh in the mind of Jesus when He spoke of Heaven as "my Father's house."

Do you have a memory like that? If you do, cherish it. If you do, thank God for it. Do you have a memory of a home that was in some small way a taste of Heaven? Are you giving somebody else a memory like that? Will it be possible for someone to think of Heaven and describe it in terms of the home you have created?

Jesus had an advantage over us. He had another memory. He had a memory of Heaven. We don't have that. Jesus had recently come from Heaven. Surely the memory of what Heaven was like never died out in His heart. We can never have that.

For me, it's impossible to read this text and not think of a little chorus I learned in church in childhood. "Everything's all right in my Father's house . . . in my Father's house . . . in my Father's house. Everything's all right in my Father's house. There is joy, joy, joy."

Have you ever flown over a city at night? Sometimes you fly low enough that you can make out the lights in individual homes. Did you ever try to imagine all the things that are going on in all those houses? In one, someone is coming home from work, tired and weary. In some, people are in the kitchen cooking supper. In others, children are doing their homework. Simple, sweet, lovable things one can picture happening in all those homes. But in how many of those brightly lit houses is there the darkness of dissension? In how many are people quarreling, criticizing, fighting? How many of those homes are breaking apart? How many husbands and wives are saying things to one another that they would never say even to a stranger, let alone a friend? In how many of those homes are the children absent and the parents unaware of where they are or what they are doing? How much heartache lies behind those little squares of light?

Compare such a scene with that chorus, "Everything's all right in my Father's house." In that house no tear is ever shed, no heart ever breaks, no pain is ever felt. That is the only place that always and ultimately deserves the name "home."

In this text there is also an appealing description. "In my Father's house are many mansions." If you read that in one of the modern versions, you will be disappointed with it. You will not find the word "mansions." You will find instead the word "rooms." That seems quite unsatisfactory to those of us who have grown up with the King James Version of the Bible. However, it is in fact the better translation. "In my Father's house are many rooms." That is really what Jesus said. But I know that they are mansions. In spite of the Greek word that is very properly translated "rooms," I know that they are mansions. I know that He who always does abundantly more than we ask or think, that He who has given us richly all things to enjoy, that He who has showered blessings indescribable in this life, has provided for us richly in the life to come. I don't need a word to tell me that!

Everything I know about God the Father tells me that. Everything I know about Jesus the Savior tells me that. Verse after verse in the Bible assures me they are mansions indeed. You may live in a tiny apartment on this earth, but you're going to have a mansion there. You may live in one small, cramped room in this life, but you're going to have a mansion there.

A tent or a cottage, why should I care,
When they're building a palace for me over there.
(Harriet E. Buell)

More than once we've all driven down the highway, bone-tired, and motel after motel has greeted us with an illuminated sign: "No Vacancy." But they will never hang a "No Vacancy" sign over the doorway to Heaven. "In my Father's house are *many* rooms." Many rooms! Christ may call His followers from every corner of the universe, from every point of the compass, from each of the four winds. It matters not how many come to Him, there will be room. They will come from every generation, from every continent, from every land. They will come home to the Father's house, and there will be room for all.

But the best part is this: Jesus said, "It's where I am." If it's where Jesus is, it doesn't matter how small the room. Just a cot in a corner will be enough if it's where Jesus is! I don't need many rooms. I don't need a mansion. I don't need golden streets or gates of pearl. If Jesus is there, that's all that's needed. We've all heard the old expression, "Home is where Mother is." That's sometimes true. Maybe you grew up with the kind of mother who could make any kind of place into a home. There is a more universally true expression, "Home is where the heart is." You may count the place where you were born as your home state or your home country. Or you may count another as your home state, or your home country. Home is where the heart is. Heaven is where Jesus is.

Some will tell you that Heaven will be right back here on Earth. A lot of us don't think that's so, but it really doesn't matter. I don't care if Heaven is on Earth, Mars, Venus, or Jupiter or on the farthest flung star in the Milky Way. Heaven is where Jesus is! That's enough. That's all we need to know.

But it is intriguing to read the description of it. Streets of gold. You may have traveled many a mile to see one golden brick. They pave the streets with them in Heaven. Ships coming to the

New World often carried much less cargo than they did on the return voyage. So they carried ballast stones to fill out the weight. When they got to the new world they discarded them. People paved the streets with them and you can see them in our older cities: Savannah, Georgia, San Juan, Puerto Rico, and others. When I think of the streets of gold, I think of those ballast stones.

When I read about Gates of Pearl, I think of the few pearls I've seen and how very small they were. Then I read about the Tree of Life. I read about the divi-divi tree long before I ever saw one. It grows on the island of Curacao in the Caribbean. All of the branches are on one side of the tree. The reason is that the trade winds blow out of the east constantly for eleven months of the year. It forms the tree in this way. I was anxious to see one. When I did, it was something of a disappointment. I don't know that I ever went so far to see so little. But the Tree of Life is not going to be a disappointment. I've heard about that tree from earliest childhood. Before I could ever identify an oak or a locust or a chestnut tree, I had heard about the Tree of Life. I've read about it all my life and I'm going to see it someday! I know it's not going to be a disappointment.

Someone once gave me a book entitled *Cities of Destiny*. Some cities just happened, and some were deliberately created. Brasilia, for example, was deliberately created in the midst of the jungle to be the new capital of Brazil. There are planned cities, and others that just grew up and sprawled out. In that book on cities of destiny, there is one conspicuously missing. That's the city where my destiny lies.

Once it was said that all roads led to Rome. But only one road leads to this city of destiny. In the very same chapter as this text, Jesus said, "I am the way. No man cometh unto the Father but by me." That chorus from childhood about the Father's house has also this verse:

Jesus is the Way to my Father's house,
  to my Father's house,
  to my Father's house.
Jesus is the Way to my Father's house.
There is joy, joy, joy!

Does Jesus Care?

The text I heard quoted most often as a child was John 11:35. I grew up in a small town where everybody was a Protestant if they were anything at all. It wasn't thought strange that the teacher in public school required you to memorize and recite a verse from the Bible every day. Every morning there was someone who forgot to do it. Having forgotten, he always fell back upon the only refuge open to him, and quoted John 11:35, "Jesus wept." This was invariably greeted with snickers of laughter.

This is, of course, a verse to be taken seriously. Few verses in the Bible are more significant. It's short enough to be sharp. "Jesus wept." Tears appear often in the biblical narrative, but nowhere more movingly than here.

The Bible never says, "Jesus laughed." I am certain that He did. He was so often a welcome guest at banquets, feasts and parties. If Jesus had been a grim, glum, sad, sour soul that would not have been the case. They said of Jesus, "He's a wine-bibber and a glutton." He was neither. The reason they thought that was they heard all the laughter coming from the house where Jesus was a guest.

Occasionally a group of ministers will be together for lunch.

Each one has a fund of stories to share, and each story is funnier than the one before. If you sat at a nearby table you'd find it hard to believe that we are all stone cold sober. It was like that with Jesus.

Another reason I think Jesus laughed is because of the humorous things Jesus said. We miss the humor because we know the punch line in advance, and that always spoils the joke. A joke turns upon a sudden perception of incongruity. But when Jesus spoke of a blind man who got another to lead him and both fell in a ditch, it was as funny as the Three Stooges. When Jesus said a man with a beam in his eye tried to get a speck out of someone else's eye, people laughed. That's funny! When He spoke of those who carefully washed the outside of the cup but not the inside, it was funny!

Another reason I think Jesus laughed is this: the person who has no sense of humor doesn't understand life. There are great slices of life that after all are really uproariously funny. If you have no sense of humor you don't understand life. Because I'm sure Jesus understood life perfectly, I'm confident He laughed. But the Bible never says, "Jesus laughed."

The Bible does say, "Jesus wept." What if the Bible did not say, "Jesus wept"? We would always have assumed that Jesus wept, but we needed to know it with certainty. We need the assurance and the reassurance that Jesus wept. The book of Hebrews calls Jesus our high priest and says, "We have not an high priest which cannot be touched with the feeling of our infirmities." It's important to know that Jesus can be touched ... that Jesus wept.

Does Jesus care when my heart is pained
Too deeply for mirth and song,
As the burdens press, and the cares distress,
And the way grows weary and long?
Oh yes, He cares; I know He cares,
His heart is touched with my grief.
(Frank E. Graeff)

One of the ways I know He cares is that Jesus wept. The occasion of this text is the death of Lazarus. Lazarus and his sisters, Mary and Martha, had been close friends of Jesus. They had often been His hosts. Jesus was away when Lazarus died. When finally He arrived, He was taken to a tomb. He wept. "Then the Jews said, "See how he loved him." We don't know why Jesus wept. The neighbors thought that Jesus wept because of His love for Lazarus. We are certain that the fact that Jesus wept is convincing proof that He loves us.

It is possible that Jesus wept out of sympathy for the sorrowing sisters. It was an interesting family: two sisters and a brother. None of them had ever married. They lived together and made a home for one another. In that culture, the brother functioned as the head of the family. Now he is dead. The two sisters are alone in the world and it is possible that Jesus wept in sympathy for them.

It's important for us to know that people sympathize with us.

Blest be the tie that binds Our hearts in Christian love;
. . . .

We share our mutual woes, Our mutual burdens bear;
And often for each other flows The sympathizing tear.
(John Fawcett)

Someone said of marriage, "May there be such a oneness between you that when one cries tears the other tastes salt." It can be like that in the household of faith, too.

When you feel sympathetic pain, the problem is in one part of the body, but the pain is felt in another part of the body. In the body of Christ we often have sympathetic pain. It means a lot to us. It means even more to know that Jesus sympathizes. When we weep, He weeps. "The Great Physician now is near, the sympathizing Jesus" (William Hunter).

It is, however, equally possible that Jesus wept because of the crowd. The crowd did not believe. Jesus knew He was going to raise Lazarus from the dead and that they still would not believe. That's how stubborn their doubt was. In fact, some say the resurrection of Lazarus provoked the crucifixion of Jesus. It convinced the opposition that Jesus had to be dealt with once and for all. So they began to conspire to kill Him. Not only that, they conspired to kill Lazarus. Disbelieving the evidence, they decided to destroy the evidence. Jesus knew all that and it may be that He wept because of the doubt of those around Him.

How do we respond to doubt? How do we respond to a disbelieving world? Sometimes we respond in anger. Sometimes we respond in panic. Jesus responded in pity.

This is not the only occasion on which Jesus wept. Once He stood on the Mount of Olives and looked across the valley at the city of Jerusalem and wept. He cried out, "O Jerusalem, Jerusalem, how often would I have gathered thy children together as a hen gathers her chickens under her wing, and ye would not." Those are indescribably sad words. "And ye would not."

I am glad that Jesus wept for an individual and I am glad that He wept for a city. I am glad that He wept for one and glad that He wept for many. Doubt caused Jesus to respond in this way because of His love. Have you ever loved someone greatly and had them doubt you? It hurts. It may not hurt much if a stranger or a casual acquaintance doubts you. But if you love somebody and they doubt you, it hurts. Because Jesus loved the world so greatly, He responded to its doubt with sorrow.

However, it is possible that we may not yet have discovered why Jesus wept. It may not have been because of His sympathy for the sisters of Lazarus. It may not have been because of the doubt of those about Him. He may have wept for Lazarus. We assume that Jesus did Lazarus a great favor when He raised him from the dead. But was that such a great favor? Lazarus is called back from Heaven to earth, from eternity back into time. He had to face again life's pain and life's problems. Now he had to face the opposition of those who would try to kill him and he had to die all over again. Perhaps Jesus wept for him.

It may be that death is not as terrible a thing as we have supposed. The Bible suggests that. Books recently published about dying experiences suggest that. It may not have been death Jesus dreaded in Gethsemane, but only the suffering on the cross that would precede death. In any case, it is possible that Jesus wept for Lazarus.

We don't know if He wept for Mary and Martha, for the crowd, or for Lazarus. But this much is sure. We know that He did not weep for himself. Self-pity was one thing in which Jesus would not indulge. We often see people mired down in self-pity.

The theme song of their lives is, "Poor Me." We recoil from self pity. We honor those who rise above it. We honor the organizations that help people rise above it. We honor the people who enter the Boston Marathon in wheelchairs. We honor blind people who consider their blindness nothing more than an inconvenience.

If any man had reason for self-pity it was Jesus. He was a wholly innocent man about to be tried, convicted, tortured and executed. The very people He himself had created were about to kill Him. He knew that some of the very people for whom He died would not understand Him and would reject him. If ever there was a person who had reason to pity himself, it was Jesus, but He wouldn't do it.

Because of the culture in which we've grown up, it particularly moves us to see a man cry, especially if it's a big muscular, stalwart man. Our culture has taught us that it is all right for women and children to cry but that men aren't supposed to cry. There is no physical basis for that. Men have tear ducts, too! But because of this strange feature of our culture it always moves us to see a man cry. I can only remember two occasions on which I saw my father cry. One was a winter day when the wind came out of the north, fierce and strong, and it blew tears out of his eyes. The other occasion was at church. The sermon had been particularly moving. Out of the corner of my eye I saw him lift that hard, calloused hand and brush away a tear. I was only a child, but it made an unforgettable impression on me.

In the Greek Orthodox Cathedral at Tarpon Springs, Florida, there is a picture of their patron saint, St. Nicholas. Such a picture is regarded as holy in the Greek Orthodox Church. A few years ago people came from far and wide to see that picture, because it wept. If you are at all familiar with the intense humidity of Florida, it is not surprising that anything under glass would weep. But to those who believed it was all very significant. They said the picture wept because St. Nicholas himself wept. They were moved by it. We may have some problem with that, but we are all touched to know that Jesus wept.

We are touched all the more to know that He weeps still. Perhaps He weeps for you and me. Perhaps some Sunday He sees an empty place at church, where you usually sit, and weeps that you are not there. You have not kept your appointment with Him there. It is possible that He looks into your life, sees some ugly sin, and weeps that you have disobeyed His will. Perhaps He listens to your conversation, hears His own name, spoken not in reverence but in profanity, and weeps. Perhaps He weeps that you would speak His name so lightly, so carelessly. The Bible says that there is joy in Heaven when one sinner repents. May we not then conclude that there is grief in Heaven whenever one sinner refuses to repent? You must decide whether you will bring a tear to the eye of Jesus or a smile to the face of God!

The Power of a Touch

In Stockholm, Sweden, a lady was pinned beneath a streetcar. She was seriously injured and bleeding badly. A crowd collected. They tried to move the streetcar, but it was too heavy. There was nothing to do but wait for the heavy equipment to come. She was in great pain. She was losing blood rapidly. Suddenly a young man broke away from the crowd. He crawled under the street car. He took the woman's hand and said, "Hold my hand tightly until help comes." In holding his hand she grew calm. She avoided going into shock. The loss of blood was slowed. Finally, after she was freed, she said, "I never knew the touch of a hand could mean so much."

Some people in the New Testament might have said that. Two of them are in Matthew 8:

When he came down from the mountainside, large crowds followed him. A man with leprosy came and knelt before him and said, "Lord, if you are willing, you can make me clean."

Jesus reached out his hand and touched the man. "I am willing," he said. "Be clean!" Immediately he was cured of his leprosy.... When Jesus came into Peter's house, he saw Peter's mother-in-law lying in bed with a fever. He touched her hand and the fever left her, and she got up and began to wait on him (Matthew 8:1-3, 14, 15, *NIV*).

These are only two of many such instances. He touched blind eyes and made them see. He touched deaf ears and they could hear. In the garden of Gethsemane Peter defended Him and wounded a servant of the high priest. Jesus touched his ear and healed him.

On the Mount of Transfiguration Jesus' garments were changed. They shone like the light. Moses and Elijah appeared, and God spoke. The disciples were afraid. Jesus touched them and said, "Do not be afraid." There was healing in His touch. There was reassurance in His touch. There was comfort in His touch. There was life in His touch.

Near the village of Nain He met a funeral procession. A widow's only son had died. Jesus touched the casket, and the dead man came back to life.

He touched people and people touched Him. A woman who had been ill for years touched the hem of His garment and was healed.

Several years ago Queen Elizabeth II visited the United States. She addressed the joint houses of Congress. She was escorted to the platform by the sergeant at arms, "Fishbait" Miller. He took her arm to help her up the steps. Cameras clicked. Flash bulbs popped. The next day the picture was in the press. Miller had committed a great breach of etiquette. Nobody touches the Queen.

Jesus Christ, King of Heaven and earth, King of *kings*, touched people. And people touched Him.

You and I will never feel the touch of that hard, calloused carpenter's hand. No one in our day is going to feel the physical touch of that hand. But they can feel His touch through your hand. They can feel His touch through my hand.

Once there was an orphanage, overcrowded and under-staffed. The children were well fed, well clothed, and well housed, but there was no time for any exchange of affection. There were no hugs or kisses. They sickened and died.

Duke McCall went to a high government official in one of the Communist countries. He went on behalf of the Baptist World

Alliance. The government was about to close one of their orphanages. The official said, "I have visited your institution. The buildings are in bad repair. The roof leaks. Much improvement needs to be done. But I am going to let you stay open. I have seen the love." He saw the love!

Those first Christians greeted one another with a holy kiss. Some have thought that was a ritual for the church, but since men kissed men and women kissed women, it never caught on. Someone asked one preacher if his church practiced the holy kiss. He said, "No, but we practice the holy hug a lot."

The kiss was the common greeting in that day. It still is in Eastern Europe. Whenever a man meets another man who is a close friend, they will kiss, first on one cheek and then on the other. When ladies meet who are friends, they will kiss one another. That's the way it was in New Testament times. But to the Christians that common greeting took on an uncommon significance. It became holy. There was another element in it. There was a new element in it.

The ordinary greeting of the street became a holy kiss. We may express it with a handclasp or a hug or a pat on the back, but the power of a touch is still there.

Once I was visiting a terminally ill patient in the intensive care unit of a hospital. The patient was no longer conscious, hut the nurse knew that the senses of hearing and touch are the last senses we lose. So she was sitting there, holding the dying patient's hand. There were no more injections that could be given. There were no more treatments that could be given. That was the only thing left to do. Nurses in intensive care units are highly trained. It is a very specialized branch of nursing. Yet, this highly trained nurse did not think it a misuse of her time to hold that patient's hand through that entire shift. She provided for that patient the last ministry she could offer: the ministry of touch.

On another occasion I was visiting a lady with cancer. When I entered the room a friend was already there. The patient was crying, and the friend was patting her and saying, "Now, now, don't cry. Everything's going to be all right." That was not true. Everything was not going to be all right and she had every reason to cry. So when the friend left, I pulled a chair up beside the bed, sat down, and just held the patient's hand. After about ten minutes she spoke: "Mr. Shannon, you're such a comfort to me." I had not said one word!

We use the word touch to mean something more than one hand upon another. We use it to mean caring. We say a certain song touched us; a sermon touched us; a story touched us. You see that here in these stories from Matthew.

It was a *leper* Jesus touched—a man nobody touched. They thought leprosy was highly contagious. Think of it! For years this man had not felt the firm handclasp of a friend, the kiss of a child, the embrace of a mate. Jesus touched *him*. He did not have to touch him to heal him. Often He healed with a command. Sometimes He healed at a distance. I deliberately omitted some verses in quoting the text. Between these two stories of the healing touch there is a third. A nobleman's servant was ill. Jesus healed him at a distance. He was not even in the same room! He was not even in the same city! He did not touch him to heal him. He touched him to show that He cared. He touched the untouchable. He cured the incurable.

Hebrews 4:15 says, "We have not a high priest which cannot be touched." Those priests of His day had become politicians and no longer shared the suffering of the people. The Greeks in that day thought the gods unmoved by the plight of humans. After all, they reasoned, if the gods feel pity for man, then man controls the gods. Jesus came as one who could be touched physically and who could be touched emotionally.

I was taught that Jesus performed His miracles to prove He was divine. That's true, of course. I was taught that they were His credentials. But that is not all of the truth. He healed because He cared. More than once the gospels say that He was "moved with compassion."

Does Jesus care when my heart is pained
Too deeply for mirth and song;
As the burdens press, and the cares distress,
And the way grows weary and long?

The chorus of that song gives an emphatic answer:

O yes, He cares; I know He cares,
His heart is touched with my grief
                    (Frank E. Graeff)

As Christ cares, so the church must care. And the world must
know that we care. Once I heard a missionary laboriously explaining why he spent so much of his time healing the sick and
feeding the hungry. He explained that one who is in pain, or
who is hungry, will not listen very closely to the gospel. I
thought his explanation unnecessary. It is enough to feed the
hungry because they are hungry. It is enough to heal the sick
because they are sick. If it is done in the name of Christ and He
gets the glory, then that is enough, whether they are ever converted or not!
We must show the world that the church cares. Perhaps we
cannot feed the starving millions, but we can feed one. And if
we can feed one we ought to feed one. If we can clothe one, we
ought to clothe one. If we can heal one, we ought to heal one.
We use the word "touch" in still a third way. We use it of
conversion. William J. Gaither's song has become a favorite of
many:

Shackled by a heavy burden,
'Neath a load of guilt and shame;
Then the hand of Jesus touched me,
And now I am no longer the same.

That fits our text. We have always thought of leprosy as an
illustration of sin. Leprosy is a disease and sin is a disease. We
think of sin as "doin' what comes naturally," but sin is a disease,
an abnormality. Leprosy was a progressive disease. First the
fingers were lost. Then the hand was lost. Then the arm was
lost. Sin is progressive. We begin with a small sin. We move then
to a larger sin. Leprosy was thought to be contagious. Sin is
contagious. If that is not so then why do we see the same sins
repeated in the same family, generation after generation after
generation? If that is not so, why are there some sections of any
city where you do not dare to go? Sin is contagious.
Leprosy was a hideous, disfiguring disease. Sin is likewise

ugly. Oh, it appears to be beautiful at that start, but that's because sin wears a mask. Beneath the mask it is hideously ugly.

"Shine, mister?" cried the aggressive shoe shine boy.

"No," snarled a businessman.

"Shine 'em so you can see your face in 'em," cried the enthusiastic boy.

"No!" snarled the man.

The boy looked up into that scowling face and said, "Can't say as I blame you."

Leprosy isolated its victims. They lived apart and were required to shout "Unclean!" when they passed through the streets. Sin isolates. It cuts one off from family, from friends. Finally sin separates a man from himself. Sin isolates us.

In one school the assistant principal was noted for her lovely voice. The children heard her every morning on the intercom. But one boy in kindergarten didn't know how a public address system works. When they asked him to name his favorite teacher he said, "The one in the little box." Sin puts us in a box.

Sin is also like leprosy because leprosy is deadly and sin is deadly. And forgiveness is like healing. Both are called cleansing!

A man once made a great change in his behavior. His friends were mystified. They asked his wife if he had changed his religion.

She said, "No, his religion has changed him."

There are days so dark that I seek in vain
For the face of my Friend divine;
But tho' darkness hide, He is there to guide
By the touch of His hand on mine.

(Jessie B. Pounds)

The Riddle of the Bread of Life

I think when I read that sweet story of old,
When Jesus was here among men,
How He called little children as lambs to His fold.
I should like to have been with Him then.

(Jemimo Luke)

That expresses the common longing of us all. We should like to have been with Him then. And, above all, we should like to have heard Him preach. We have only three of His sermons left to us. That's surprising. We have many parables and countless conversations, but only three sermons. One of them is the focus of our attention here. It's the sermon in John 6; His sermon on the bread of life.

This is the sermon Jesus preached on the morning after—the morning after the day in which He fed five thousand; the morning after the night in which He walked on the water and calmed the sea. The crowd found Him on the other side of the lake. He surprised them and He surprises us. They wanted more bread and fish. Today He refused to do what He was so ready to do the day before. Instead, He preached a sermon. In that sermon are three riddles that tell us three aspects of His nature.

The first riddle is in verse 27: "Do not work for food that spoils, but for food that endures to eternal life, which the Son of Man will give you." There is a bread that never grows stale. The second riddle is in verse 35: "I am the bread of life. He who comes to me will never go hungry, and he who believes in me will never be thirsty." There is a bread that ever satisfies. The third is in verse 51: "I am the living bread that came down from heaven. If a man eats of this bread, he will live forever" *(NIV)*. There is a bread that gives eternal life.

Let us look at the first riddle: the bread that never grows stale. All bread grows stale. Jesus means to get our attention so that we may learn about Him.

A couple used to come to me after church some Sundays and complain that the Communion bread had gone stale. I always thought it was something else that had gone stale! Some of our religious neighbors say that weekly Communion makes the bread go stale. It is interesting that they never apply this reasoning to anything else: to prayer or Bible reading or giving. No one says the less often you pray the more meaningful prayer will be; the less you read the Bible the more it will mean to you; the less you give the more significant stewardship will be to you. The reasoning is applied only to Communion. And it is not applied to Communion by people who have experienced weekly Communion, but rather by people who have never done so. We who have had it weekly all our lives give a different testimony. It means more to us with each Sunday that passes. It never grows stale.

But the reason that Communion bread never grows stale is that Christ never grows old. We sing of the old, old story but it really is always a new, new story. His sermons sound as if they were preached yesterday. His parables seem to have been drawn from modern life. His conversations would fit a modern man. That's why we never tire of singing about Him, reading about Him, speaking about Him.

My earliest memory of my mother is of her reading the Bible. My latest memory of my mother is of her reading the Bible. Even when her eyes were dim, she'd get out a magnifying glass and peer at the page every night. She grew old reading the Word of God, but the Word of God never grew old.

And we never tire of serving Him. Isn't that a lovely song that says, "The longer I serve him the sweeter he grows"?

Then there is a bread that ever satisfies. Fame doesn't satisfy. Money doesn't satisfy. Success doesn't satisfy. Pleasure doesn't satisfy. But there is a bread that ever satisfies.

Jesus did not describe himself as the cake of life but as the bread of life. You can grow tired of cake. I knew once an executive who traveled a lot. He stayed in the best hotels and ate at the best restaurants. He said to me, "Do you know you can get tired of eating steak?" We grow tired of the exotic foods of life, but we never grow tired of bread.

Now some don't eat bread anymore. It's not on their diet. We forget that bread is still the principal food of most of the world as it has been for most of history. Bread satisfies.

He satisfies us intellectually. We want to know about man. We learn from Jesus, the perfect man. We want to know about God. Jesus said, "He who has seen me has seen the Father." Stanislaw Lem, a Polish scientist and the author of forty books, an atheist, says, "In my thinking is a terrible hole which I cannot fill with anything."

G. K. Chesterton said something similar. "I had found this hole in the world," he said. But Chesterton came to faith in God and Jesus Christ and wrote that, "the dogma fitted exactly into the hole in the world." He satisfies us intellectually.

He satisfies us emotionally. What are the hungers of the heart? Security. Acceptance. Love. Peace. Contentment.

When Shah Jehan of India had completed the world's most beautiful building, the Taj Mahal, he dedicated it to his beloved wife and put on the cornerstone, "To the Memory of an Undying Love." But the love of Christ is more than a memory. It's a present reality.

He satisfies us spiritually. The Batonga, in the Zambezi valley of Africa, had a tradition about God before the missionaries came, but it didn't satisfy. One version was that a woman threshing grain with mortar and pestle had lifted the long pole too high and struck God in the face. It made Him angry and He went away. He never came back. Another version was that a man wiped his dirty hands on the sky. It made God angry and he went away. He never came back. How vastly different is the

God we come to know in Christ, and how infinitely more satisfying.

He satisfies all of us. We sing, "Bread of the world in mercy broken." And it is indeed the bread of the world. Think of all the different kinds of bread in the world: the flat bread of Scandinavia, the risen scones of Scotland, the light white bread of America, the dark rye of Germany, the black bread of Russia, the gray bread of Yugoslavia, the yellow cornbread of the American south, the hard rolls of Austria and the soft croissants of France. But here in Communion bread we find the one bread for the whole world.

I have received it from the hand of a deacon, an usher, an elder, and from the hand of a fellow worshiper, but I always felt that I really received it from the hand of Christ and it was always the same bread.

I have eaten it leavened and unleavened, broken it from a loaf and broken it from a wafer and had it served pre-broken, but it was always the same bread, the bread of remembrance, the bread of the world. It has been broken in the islands of the South Seas where each Lord's Day begins. Our brothers and sisters have eaten it in Australia and New Zealand, "under the Southern Cross." The table has been spread in India in the shadows of a thousand towering idols, in Africa beneath thatched huts, in Europe behind the Iron Curtain (sometimes secretly, sometimes openly), and in Britain in great cathedrals and in tiny house churches. It is the bread of the world because He is the universal Christ.

For Jesus Christ is the man for all seasons; the man for all societies. He is also the man for all stations in life. Once the Duke of Wellington, honored as a hero after the battle of Waterloo, worshiped in a small church in England. It was their custom to kneel at the front for Communion and naturally they brought the Duke of Wellington forward in the first wave. Just then the back door opened and a drunk staggered in. He was dirty and his clothes were ragged. Somewhere long ago he too had knelt like that to receive Communion and the memory of it stirred in his foggy brain. So he stumbled forward and knelt right beside the Duke of Wellington. Someone took his arm and whispered, "Move over! That's the Duke of Wellington."

But the Duke put his gloved hand on the dirty sleeve and said, "Stay where you are. There are no dukes here."

There is a bread that gives eternal life. It is not common bread. That only sustains us for a few hours. It is not Communion bread. We place no wafer on the lips of the dying. It is the Christ, for whom the bread stands. He gives eternal life.

Years ago a deacon I knew was asked to be an elder. He was reluctant to do so. He didn't consider it a promotion. He said, "I like being a deacon. When I pass the bread I feel that I am handing people the bread of life." It was a beautiful sentiment and it was poetically correct, but theologically it was wrong. Communion bread is not the bread of life. Jesus himself is the bread of life. Because He lives, we too shall live. We do not simply eat this bread in His memory. We do not simply eat this bread in His honor. We eat this bread in His presence!

On Easter Sunday we broke this bread behind the Iron Curtain. There were twelve of us. I recalled that there were also twelve in the upper room the very first time this bread was broken. My wife said, "No, we are not twelve here, but thirteen." She was right, of course. There were only twelve you could see; only twelve you could count. But we were not twelve, we were thirteen. The promise made so long ago was kept. The living Christ was in the midst. He broke the bread with us.

Florida was first explored by Europeans searching for the fountain of youth. They never found it. Romania also had a legend of a realm of "youth without age." Recently a Romanian doctor, Ana Aslan, has been trying to make the dream come true with her controversial drugs Gerovital and Aslavital. I have traveled widely in Romania and seen no evidence that she has found the fountain of youth.

I saw a cartoon once that showed a couple in mid-life strolling through a garden. The husband is saying, "Well, I guess finding the fountain of middle age was better than nothing." But there is no fountain of youth and there is no fountain of middle age and death stalks us all.

Beneath the Capuchin Church in Vienna, in the crypt of the Hapsburg emperors, lies the tomb of Carl VI, decorated with a crown, but the crown rests on a skull. Near Baden in Austria is the Heiligenkreuz monastery. In one room the walls are covered with pictures of the Babenberger emperors, but behind and above them stands Father Time.

There is a bread that gives eternal life. Jesus deliberately startled His hearers by saying, "Except you eat my flesh and drink my blood you have no life in you." He knew what they thought of cannibalism. He deliberately shocked them to get their attention. But He did not mean flesh and blood at all. Communion bread is not magically changed to flesh nor is Communion wine magically changed to blood.

He spoke of himself. He gave a new definition to bread and a new definition to life. As bread is assimilated into the body, Jesus must be assimilated into the mind and heart and life. We are to think His thoughts. We are to feel His emotions. His deeds are to be our deeds. In this way He becomes to us the bread of everlasting life.

It is not the miracle bread He'd made the day before. It is not the memorial bread on the Communion table. It is Christ himself. "I am the living bread that came down from heaven. If anyone eats of this bread, he will live forever."

I should like to have tasted the manna that came down from Heaven. I should like to have eaten of the loaves from which He fed five thousand. I should like to have received the broken bread from His own hand in the upper room. But He has provided something far better for us all.

Bread of heav'n, on Thee we feed,
For Thy flesh is meat indeed; . . .
Day by day, with strength supplied
Thro' the life of Him who died,
Ever let our souls be fed
With this true and living bread.
                                    (J. Conder)

Ten lepers + their sin

And Then There Were Nine

Some of the questions Jesus asked go straight to the heart.
One is found in the seventeenth chapter of the Gospel of Luke:

And it came to pass, as he went to Jerusalem, that he passed
through the midst of Samaria and Galilee. And as he entered
into a certain village, there met him ten men that were lepers,
which stood afar off: and lifted up their voices, and said,
Jesus, Master, have mercy on us. And when he saw them, he
said unto them, Go show yourselves unto the priests. And it
came to pass that, as they went, they were cleansed. And one
of them, when he saw that he was healed, turned back, and
with a loud voice glorified God, and fell down on his face at
his feet, giving him thanks: and he was a Samaritan. And
Jesus answering said, Were there not ten cleansed? but where
are the nine? There are not found that returned to give glory to
God, save this stranger. And he said unto him, Arise, go thy
way: thy faith hath made thee whole.

Where are the nine? Don't you think that question might have
brought a flush of emotion to the disciples? Doesn't it do the
same for us?

I want to begin with the misfortune that is written large in this story. There were ten men who had leprosy. We have a new name for it now. We call it Hanson's disease. We have a cure for it now. There was none in Jesus' day. It was thought that there would never be a cure for this disease. It is a disease that untreated grows progressively worse. Eventually the extremities of the body are deformed. Sometimes they disappear altogether and one is left without hands or feet, and if he should survive long enough, without arms or legs. The ultimate relief from leprosy was death.

It was this to which these ten unfortunate men looked forward: increasing pain, a decreasing usefulness of the body, eventual death. Leprosy, because it was misunderstood in Jesus' day, was thought to be highly contagious. We now know that that is not so. But they thought it was so. Every leper was required to announce his coming by shouting, "Unclean!" Wouldn't you like to have that burden, whenever you met any person, to announce in a loud voice your own misfortune and warn him to stay away?

These lepers, seeing Jesus, stood afar off. We don't know how far off, but if the wind was blowing, they were required to stand at least 50 yards away. So, if it were a windy day, they stood at a distance of 150 feet, not daring to come any closer.

It had been years since one of these men had known what it was to have a firm handshake or an encouraging arm placed about his shoulders. It had been years since anyone of them had known the embrace of a wife or the kiss of a child.

Is it any wonder that there has always seemed to be a similarity between leprosy and sin? Sin has often been referred to as "the leprosy of the soul." What loneliness sin brings to people! How it cuts them off from God, from their fellow men, from those they love. How contagious it is! How progressive its course! How deadly its outcome!

But there is something else about this misfortune that intrigues us. That misfortune has brought together some people who ordinarily wouldn't be together at all. Jesus is in the border country between Galilee and Samaria. At least one of these lepers is a Samaritan. The Jews and the Samaritans had no dealings with each other. They had not for hundreds of years.

114

The Jews regarded the Samaritans as traitors who had fallen in with other nations and had mixed their pure blood with the blood of others. They had no dealings with them. That's why there was such astonishment when Jesus talked to the Samaritan woman by Jacob's well. He did the thing others never did. Here we have misfortune breaking down the barriers. Isn't that often the case?

I have read that sometimes when there is a flood or a forest fire, animals will join together peacefully that ordinarily are enemies. I don't know whether that is so or not. I have read that it is so. The natural enmity that might exist between certain animals is forgotten in the awful danger of a flood or a forest fire. Certainly we know that when war or calamity strikes the human race, the petty differences that divide us are forgotten. The trivial barriers are overlooked. It's a shame that misfortune has to accomplish what good fortune ought to accomplish.

We ought to be brought together because we have all been blessed by the Savior. Because we know Christ and love Him; because of the good things that have happened to us. These ought to be the things that unite us. How sad it is that men are more united by misfortune than they are by good fortune.

We are drawn at once from that part of the scene to this: the remarkable ingratitude of nine men who had just been healed of an incurable disease and who did not come back to thank the healer. What are the roots of their ingratitude? I think we can guess at them. When Jesus asked, "Where are the nine?" He was not asking for information. He knew exactly where every one of them was. We can only guess, but I don't think our guesses are going to be very far wrong.

Is it not safe to suppose that at least one of the nine had gone to celebrate? He'd gone to the local bar to get good and drunk in celebration of his having been healed! Or else he had gone to one of the local brothels to celebrate his healing in that way. Would we be far wrong to guess that at least one of the nine was ungrateful because of sin? Sin blocked the natural stream of thankfulness and gratitude.

Certainly we would be very harsh if we were to guess that was the case with all of them. So, we must assume that some of them were not on such errands at all. Some of them may have been ungrateful simply because they chose the good instead of the best. It's a choice we all often make.

Is it not fair to suppose that one of them said, "I must see to the affairs of my business. When I got this disease I left it in the hands of my brother-in-law and everybody knows how incompetent he is. I'm going to have to hurry to make sure that my brother-in-law has not driven my business into bankruptcy."

Nobody can argue with a concern for business. Perhaps there were employees who depended upon the success of his business for their own welfare. Perhaps if his business failed, there would be children who would go hungry or be homeless. Is it not a good thing for people to be concerned with their business? Can we find fault with a man who is concerned about it? We can if it takes precedence over more important things in life! He chose something good. He might have chosen something better.

Perhaps another said, "I've got to find an old friend; a friend I have not been able to talk with all these years. I've not felt his handshake for a decade. I'm going to look up my old friend and we're going to establish that broken friendship again."

Was there not another who said, "I'm going home to my wife and to my children. How often I've longed to feel the embrace of my wife. How often I've longed to feel the kisses of my children. I'm going home." Who can argue with that? Isn't it a good thing to want to go home? Isn't it a gold thing to cherish family ties, to love wife or husband, to love our children, to want to be with them? Isn't that good? Indeed it is. In choosing the good, he missed the best.

Perhaps there was another who said, "I'm going to do exactly what Jesus told me to do. I'm going to go to the priest and show him that I am cleansed." Under the Old Testament law, the priest was not only the religious leader, he was also the public health officer. While there was no cure for leprosy, sometimes there was a strange remission in that disease. So, there was a provision in the Old Testament law that if a leper entered remission, then he could go to the priest who as the public health officer would certify that he was free from leprosy. Then he could rejoin the human race. He no longer had to announce himself with the cry, "Unclean!" He no longer had to stay fifty yards away from everyone else.

116

There was probably a man who was doing exactly what the law said. He was a stickler for that. Today he'd say, "If it says 55 miles per hour, you don't drive 60. You never go through on the caution light. You go through on the green." It's a fine thing to be concerned about the technicalities of the law. We're all better off because there are citizens so conscious of their duty. He chose something good, but he might have chosen something better.

Would it be fair, also, to guess that there was someone among the nine who went on one of these errands out of pure thoughtlessness? It just never occurred to him to go back and say, "Thank you" to the man who healed him. If someone had mentioned it, he would have said, "That's a great suggestion. I'll do it. What a fine idea. I don't know why I didn't think of it myself." Pure thoughtlessness and simple neglect may have been responsible.

But don't you catch a note of sadness in this question? Don't you think Jesus was hurt when He asked, "Where are the nine?" When we've examined the roots of ingratitude, then perhaps we're ready to examine the fruits of ingratitude.

You can see the fruits in the life of a nation. Did you ever wonder why in the middle of the Ten Commandments there is that one that seems so out of place, "Honor thy father and mother?" That doesn't seem to fit in with, "Thou shalt not kill," "Thou shalt not steal," "Thou shalt not commit adultery," "Thou shalt not bear false witness." It seems to belong in a different category. Why is something that is a mere matter of courtesy included among these basic moral laws of life? Have you ever wondered about that? Has that commandment ever seemed to you strangely out of place among the ten? Perhaps we can understand it if we get the full verse—"Honor thy father and mother that thy days may be long in the land which the Lord thy God giveth thee." The reason is there. It is not the reason that might at first appear.

When I lived in Tennessee I knew a man who was nearing 100 years of age. People used to ask him, "How did you live to be so old? What's your recipe for a long life?" He would quote the verse that I've just quoted. He said, "I honored my father and mother and that's the reason I've lived to be such an old man." He misunderstood the verse. The verse is no guarantee of longevity. I cannot promise you that if you honor your father and mother you'll live to be 100, or 80, or even 75.

Listen to it again. "Honor thy father and mother that thy days may be long *in the land* which the Lord thy God giveth thee." He was talking about the nation, not the individual. God was saying, "This nation can survive and be strong only so long as this commandment is kept." When this commandment is disregarded, then the foundations of the nation are weakened. You can see that! It's crystal clear! We know precisely why this is among the ten commandments. National survival depends upon gratitude. He who is ungrateful makes a poor citizen. Poor citizens make a poor nation.

We see the fruits of it in family life. Shakespeare said, "How sharper than a serpent's tooth to have a thankless child." A lot of parents feel unappreciated. If you wonder about the frustrations that sometimes seem to grip them, that may be the reason. If you wonder why they sometimes lash out unexpectedly, that may be the reason. If you wonder why their punishment seems unjust or their attitude unfair, that may be the reason. A lot of parents feel unappreciated.

It would do us all good to remember that once there was a time in life when one week of neglect would have killed us.

If parents feel unappreciated, so do children. Children feel their good points are overlooked and their bad points are magnified. They feel that the spotlight is always turned on the times they do wrong and never on the times they do right. They think that they get the blame they deserve but never the credit that they deserve.

The world is also filled with wives and husbands who feel unappreciated. In family life the fruit of our ingratitude is everywhere and bitter. If people only realized how much they are appreciated. If only we could stop being so tongue-tied about the way we really feel! If we could stop being so embarrassed and express ourselves!

You see that fruit also in personal life. The nine missed the chance to praise. Worship, at its heart, is thanksgiving. Read the Psalms. There is praise for God in every page. Yet the Psalms is a book of worship. Look through the hymnal and you will find praise and thanksgiving everywhere.

When Jesus gave us the Lord's supper, what did He do? He gave thanks. If I call upon someone to pray for the offering, what do I ask them to do? To give thanks. It is at the very heart of worship. Something is lost in personal life when we lose the sense of gratitude. It spills over into all the rest of life too, so that thoughtlessness becomes a habit.

Forgetfulness becomes a way of life. There are spiritual dangers untold in that. If we no longer know how to remember and if we can no longer be thoughtful, how can we be the kind of Christians we ought to be? Sooner or later we will become thoughtless concerning God's blessings. He who is thoughtless about God's blessings will sooner or later be thoughtless about God's commands. He who is thoughtless about God's commands will sooner or later be thoughtless about God. Do you see where the road leads and how swiftly it may be traveled?

There is also here a note of gratitude. One came back and he ought not to be neglected. He ought not be ignored in turning our attention upon the nine. Gratitude may be one of the most helpful lessons we ever learn. It is one of the easiest lessons we learn. Yet, it is seldom learned. That's amazing. Something that could mean so much to us and could be learned so easily is, in fact, so seldom learned. Here the gratitude comes from the most unexpected source—a Samaritan. A Samaritan comes back to fall on his face in the dust before a Jew, thank Him, and praise God. How amazing!

Have you ever seen faith in unexpected places? I have. Have you ever seen courage where you did not expect to find it? I have. Have you ever seen character and holiness in an expected life? I have. Countless are the times I have gone out to comfort some sick person and they have comforted me instead. How often I have gone to strengthen someone else and they have strengthened me instead.

How often our best predictions have failed. Often we think of people who perhaps ought to be members of our church or are "prospective" members of our church. We try to guess which ones are going to become members of our church and which ones will not. Our guesses are generally wrong. Every time we have an evangelistic effort, I have a long list of people. I make a list of people I *know* are going to respond, and another list of people I *think* are going to respond, and another list of people I know are not going to respond. It never works out the way I think it will.

When people become members of our church there are some we think will be strong vital working members and others we figure won't last two weeks. How often we are wrong. Often we look at marriages and think, "This marriage does not have a chance." It lasts and lasts and lasts. We lock at another and say, "This marriage was surely made in Heaven and will last forever." And we are wrong. We look at young people and say, "There's a young person who is going to accomplish things and there's one who is going to get into trouble." How often we are wrong.

It ought to teach us to be more patient with everybody and it ought to teach us to be more diligent and more exacting with ourselves.

Let me ask you a question. If you had been among the ten lepers who were healed, would you have been among the nine who went their way, or would you have been the one who came back to praise God? Only you know the answer to that question. But you know. In the asking of it, there is the opportunity for all of us to become ourselves the best person we can be. That's the way we pay our debt of gratitude to God.

Troubled Hearts and Trusting Hearts
(John 14:1-6)

In this text there are two kinds of hearts: troubled hearts and trusting hearts. Physically, there are many kinds of hearts: fast hearts, slow hearts, unsteady hearts, fibrillating hearts, irregular hearts, leaking hearts, enlarged hearts. Spiritually, there are only two kinds of hearts: troubled hearts and trusting hearts. Which is yours?

Hearts are troubled by many things. Hearts are troubled by grief. How often we see a tear in someone's eye! Seeing it, we know that it has come to the surface like the mist that rises from a pond. We know that the tear in the eye bespeaks a deeper reservoir of sorrow in the heart. When one finds a mountain spring he knows that that little stream of water bespeaks a pool of water unseen beneath the ground. A tear is the token of a great pool of grief that troubles hearts, not only at the moment, but sometimes across the years. Much pain may come to us from a fresh wound. There is also the deeper pain of old sorrows.

One man was past the age of eighty. We talked about the death of his son, who had succumbed to disease in childhood. "I accept the fact that he had to die," he said, "but I have always wondered why he had to suffer so." And as he spoke, a mist came over his eyes. I was seeing a sorrow that was fifty years old. The pain, the grief, was still there.

Hearts are troubled by loneliness. It is not just seen in people who must live alone. There are people still living with their families, living on a busy street, and working every day among other people who feel a loneliness indescribable and painful.

Hearts are troubled by an uncertain future. What lies ahead? What lies ahead for the world? For civilization? For humanity? What lies ahead for my country? What lies ahead for my family? What lies ahead for me?

We don't know what one day may bring forth. We cannot chart a single moment of the future. We are not absolutely sure what we are going to do this afternoon. We may think that we know. We may have our plans. But the future is always uncertain. Sometimes it is bright with promise, sometimes it is dark with dread, but always it is uncertain. That troubles men's hearts.

Hearts are troubled by the sudden changes that are thrust upon us. There are unexpected changes, undesired changes, changes over which we have no control. Such changes threaten us. Yet life has the habit of suddenly veering off in a new direction we'd never even thought about. That troubles men's hearts.

Hearts are troubled by death. We know that that is something we are going to do, and we don't want to do it. We don't know what it feels like to die. That which lies beyond death is so mysterious. We cherish every reassurance we can find, but daily we are under the threat of death. We hear of the death of someone who is just our age. A close friend or a relative dies. At every turn in life we are reminded that death is a part of living and it troubles us.

Hearts are troubled by guilt. There is sometimes an uncertainty as to whether or not we are really right with God. Is the old account really settled? That troubles some hearts. Their sins seem larger than others' sins! They expected more of themselves. Regret, remorse, and guilt trouble hearts.

And almost all of these emotions are in the hearts of those to whom Jesus spoke. They were feeling that very night almost every one of these troubling anxieties. Grief! Jesus is going away. Where He is going they cannot go. He has made it plain enough that He is going to die, but their minds reject it. They cannot accept it.

A deep grief has filled their hearts. They know that they are facing now a loneliness that they are not at all prepared to face. For more than three years they have been with Jesus constantly. They have gone where He wished to go. They have listened to what He wanted to say. Then they have gone out to represent Him when He asked them to. He has been directing their lives daily for more than three years. Now they must be parted ... from Him and from one another. How lonely they are going to be without the presence of the Master.

They are thinking of how uncertain the future is. They thought they had it all mapped out. They thought they had figured out exactly what Jesus was going to do. They thought He'd set up an earthly kingdom. They'd sit at His right hand and at His left. They'd have positions of honor and responsibility in a new kingdom more glorious than David's. They had it all mapped out and now they begin to see that they had it all wrong. The map they made must now be crumpled up and thrown away.

What will the future hold for them? Will they go back to their old occupations—fishing and tax collecting? How can they go back? How can they admit that they have wasted three and one-half years of life on a foolish and fruitless adventure? They must face all the people who laughed at them and said, "You're a fool to follow that carpenter while there are fish to be caught and taxes to be collected." They must now go back (so they think) and admit what fools they are. How uncertain is their future!

How shattering is the change now thrust upon them. They thought they were going to give their lives to high spiritual endeavors and it looks now as if those spiritual challenges were unreal.

Death itself threatens them now. Jesus is in danger. They know it well. They refuse to accept that He is going to die, yet they know that the moment He sets foot in Judea, He walks into the very nest of His enemies. They know there is a plot already laid to kill Jesus. They know that the plot includes Lazarus. If the enemies of Jesus want to kill the man He raised from the dead, how safe are they?

Will not the enemies of Jesus want to make a clean sweep of it? Will they not want to clear out the whole nest at once? Will they be satisfied to destroy Jesus and let His disciples go? That can hardly have seemed likely to them. We have the evidence of it when they started on this very journey toward Jerusalem. Thomas said, "Let us also go and die with Him." Whatever they do not know, this they know with certainty—Jesus has walked into the very face of His enemies. Surely they know that they are as vulnerable as He. The threat of death is hot upon them.

Would it be going too far to say that some pangs of guilt stirred in their hearts, too? Can we not suppose that these good and noble men thought they ought to have been better? Did not they realize already that truth that would later be written down, "To know to do good and do it not is sin?" Are they not thinking that they should have persuaded Jesus not to come to Jerusalem? Do they not regret having quarreled so much among themselves? Didn't they think that they ought to have been wiser and better and more loyal? Is it not fair to say that that troubling thought of guilt was in their minds this dark night? And isn't there a comfort in *that?*

If the eleven best men on earth had troubled hearts, should I be surprised if mine is troubled, too? Should you? Isn't it the most natural thing in the world to have a troubled heart? Wouldn't it be strange if we did not? Do we need to punish ourselves because our hearts are troubled? I think not. If men like Andrew and Peter and James and John had troubled hearts, who am I to think that I should escape it? It is a perfectly natural thing to feel.

But beyond that there is this encouraging note. We do not have to continue to feel it. Jesus implies that we are in control. "*Let not* your heart be troubled." Our emotions are not beyond our control. They are not subject to every wind of circumstance that may blow. We are in the driver's seat. So while we need feel no guilt when our hearts are troubled, we have a remedy and do not have to go on through life with troubled hearts.

There is another alternative. "Let not your heart be troubled!" Don't let it happen to you. Don't let the circumstances of life shrivel your soul and warp your life. But you cannot accomplish this alone. So we must come to the second kind of heart—trusting hearts. "Ye believe in God, believe also in me. In my Father's house are many mansions." There you have it: faith in God, faith in Christ, faith in the future.

There is a difference between faith and trust. Faith is the root and trust is the tree and peace is both the flower and the fruit. As the root differs from the tree, so faith differs from trust. Faith has one long taproot. It reaches down to God, the basic fact, the indisputable fact. Everybody knows this fact; even the man who will not admit that he knows it. There is a God! That touches the deep taproot of faith. But reaching out to sustain that tree of trust are the feeder roots.

"Believe also in me," said Jesus. "If it were not so, I would have told you." Both the love and the character of Jesus come into play. Christ is too honest to let His followers go on believing a lie. He is too honest to let them give their lives to an illusion.

If some friend of yours set out one morning with a shovel over his shoulder intent on digging up the pot of gold at the end of the rainbow, you'd try to stop him. You'd tell him there is no end of the rainbow, and no pot of gold to be found. You'd tell him quickly that it's only a dream or an illusion. You'd never let a friend go out on such a foolish errand as that.

That's the point here. "If it were not so, I would have told you." The honest, kind, loving Jesus will not let them go on believing a lie, cherishing an illusion. And faith in Him is the feeder root of our faith.

Then He calls us to look to the future. "In my Father's house are many mansions." Notice that God is still "Father." Even when the cross is looming up ahead in all its ugliness, God is still "Father." Think of that! "My Father's house!" Think of that! Remember the prodigal son? He was far from home feeding swine when he remembered his father's house.

Jesus is talking about Heaven, but he calls it the Father's house.

"I go to prepare a place for you." Jesus knew where He was going. When I come down to die, I want to know where I am going. Don't you?

A man and his wife were driving down the highway. She said, "I think we're on the wrong road." He said, "I know we are. I'm not sure where this road is going." She said, "Then why don't you stop and turn around?" He said, "I would, but we're making such good time." That's the world. People don't know where they are going, but they certainly are making good time.

The disciples knew where they were going. The immediate future may have been hazy and indistinct, but the ultimate future was certain. They were going home—home to the Father's house. Their ultimate future was certain and sure. Don't we stand in the same place with them? We don't know the future and yet we do. Of the immediate future we know nothing. The ultimate future we know with certainty.

Faith leads to knowledge. "Whither I go ye know and the way ye know." Faith leads to obedience. "I am the way, the truth, and the life."

A man preached a sermon once on the interesting subject, "Believing Something When You Can't Believe Everything." At times the circumstances of life conspire to rob us of some of our faith. If we cherish what faith we have, it will endure ... and spread. It will be like the strawberry plant. It sends runners out in every direction. They make new strawberry plants all around. So faith sends out its runners to make new faith, in some springtime of the soul. If you can't believe everything, believe something! Cherish it. Let it grow and reproduce and develop and spread.

Now let me go back for a moment to this little company of eleven men who heard this most magnificent of all promises. Let us see if it blessed them as it blesses us. One of them, John, wrote a letter that has been preserved for us. We call it the first epistle of John. In the first chapter and the seventh verse he wrote, "The blood of Jesus Christ his Son cleanseth us from all sin." Doesn't that remove the troubling thoughts of guilt that plague us? In the second chapter he wrote, "And the world passeth away, and the lust thereof: but he that doeth the will of God abideth forever" (1 John 2:17). Does not that speak to the uncertainties of life? And in 1 John 4:15 it says, "Whosoever shall confess that Jesus is the Son of God, God dwelleth in him." Does that ease the troubling loneliness of life? God dwelleth in him!

Again in 1 John 4:8, "In this was manifested the love of God toward us, because that God sent his only begotten Son into the world, that we might live through him." *Live* through him! Does not that remove our fear of death? And in chapter five, verse eleven, "And this is the record, that God hath given to us eternal life, and this life is in His Son." How can we grieve overmuch in the face of that? And in the fifth chapter and the fourth verse, "For whatsoever is born of God overcometh the world: and this is the victory that overcometh the world, even our faith."

Life may be filled with change, but this remains constant—the victory of faith. Perhaps you have written lines like these. Perhaps you have moved from the people of the troubled heart to the congregation of the trusting heart. If you have not, you can—and should—now!

The Woman Who Came in From the Cold

Step into my time machine. It will whisk you effortlessly across the years and across the miles. We get into the time machine in the twentieth century. We step out of the time machine in the first century in the land of the Bible.

Night has fallen. The streets are quiet. In this time and place people do not go out into the streets at night unless they have business. It is not always safe. We walk down the streets and listen to the murmur of voices from the rooftops. People have gathered on the rooftops to enjoy the cool of the evening, much as we might gather on our porch or patio. Occasionally through the tiny, barred window of a home we may see the little light of an oil lamp and someone moving back and forth.

What's that? There is someone on the street; someone there in the shadows! It's a woman! Why is *she* here alone on the streets at night? We no more ask the question than we know the answer. We have seen her kind in our own time and place and we know why she is here. We hurry on.

We move into a better part of town. The houses are built around courtyards. We can look through the gates into the open courtyards and see fires glowing and people gathered about them talking and eating.

As we pass through this better section of the village we begin to hear sounds louder than any we have heard from other homes. There, that's where they are coming from; from that house over there! We stop and peer through the gates. A banquet is in progress. A crowd has gathered in the courtyard. It is easy to see the head table and the guest of honor. They sit in the Roman fashion, reclining on the left elbow, their legs bent at the knees, their feet behind them.

Suddenly someone brushes past us at the gate and goes into the courtyard. Who is this party-crasher? We recognize her. It's the woman we saw moments before on the street. What's *she* doing here?

Carefully she makes her way around the crowd so as to be unobserved. She comes up behind the head table. She comes up behind the guest of honor. What can she be doing? She is opening up a bottle of perfume and pouring it on His feet. And then she weeps uncontrollably, washing His feet with her tears.

That's the dramatic story that the Bible tells in Luke 7:36-50.

Now one of the Pharisees invited Jesus to have dinner with him, so he went to the Pharisee's house and reclined at the table. When a woman who had lived a sinful life in that town learned that Jesus was eating at the Pharisee's house, she brought an alabaster jar of perfume, and as she stood behind him at his feet weeping, she began to wet his feet with her tears. Then she wiped them with her hair, kissed them and poured perfume on them.

When the Pharisee who had invited him saw this, he said to himself, "If this man were a prophet, he would know who is touching him and what kind of woman she is—that she is a sinner."

Jesus answered him, "Simon, I have something to tell you."

"Tell me, teacher," he said.

"Two men owed money to a certain moneylender. One owed him five hundred denarii, and the other fifty. Neither of them had the money to pay him back, so he canceled the debts of both. Now which of them will love him more?"

Simon replied, "I suppose the one who had the bigger debt canceled."

"You have judged correctly," Jesus said.

Then he turned toward the woman and said to Simon, "Do you see this woman? I came into your house. You did not give me any water for my feet, but she wet my feet with her tears and wiped them with her hair. You did not give me a kiss, but this woman, from the time I entered, has not stopped kissing my feet. You did not put oil on my head, but she has poured perfume on my feet. Therefore, I tell you, her many sins have been forgiven—for she loved much. But he who has been forgiven little loves little."

Then Jesus said to her, "Your sins are forgiven."

The other guests began to say among themselves, "Who is this who even forgives sins?"

Jesus said to the woman, "Your faith has saved you; go in peace." *(NIV)*

We are certain that she did go in peace. That night she experienced the only peace that she had known for years—the peace of knowing that sins are forgiven.

We can identify with her because we too are sinners. All of us have sinned and come short. They criticized Jesus for eating with sinners. Let me ask you, who else was there with whom He might eat? If He didn't eat with sinners, He would eat with no one. All of us are sinners. We identify with her.

Our sins are different than hers. They are less scandalous, less public. We like to divide sin into big sins and little sins, as our Catholic neighbors divide them into mortal sins and venial sins and as the law divides them into felonies and misdemeanors. So we like to divide them into crimes and little peccadillos. Of course it is easy to tell the big sins from the little sins. My sins are the little sins and your sins are the big sins. But the Bible knows no such distinctions. It refuses to grade or categorize sins. It simply puts them all together and labels us all as sinners.

Because she was a sinner she had felt shut out by life. When you think about it, the one person in society who never ̵n friend is a prostitute. She may have enemies—the law have clients. She may have competitors in other pr̵ she never has a friend.

Perhaps for different reasons, you too ha̵

life. You have felt a sense of loneliness. You have felt that you somehow did not belong. Jesus comes to say to you as He said to her, "You do belong."

We can identify with her because we too are often troubled by conscience.

We're on a collision course in life. Good and evil, light and darkness, Heaven and Hell are all on a collision course. You and I are caught in the middle. We experience, as she did, the pangs of conscience. That's what brought forth her tears. She wept out of a deep, deep sense of regret. She wished that she was not the person that she was. She had never intended to be what she was. She had drifted into this life. She had had other plans for herself. She had never imagined that she would find herself in this position. One day she woke up and said, "How did I get to be where I am today? Is there any way to get out of the position I'm in today?" And deep regret swept over her. It was tears of regret that she shed at the feet of Jesus.

Repentance does not just look back and say, "I'm sorry." It also looks ahead at the possibilities of the future and says, "Wow!" We need to bring that "Wow" element into repentance. Repentance is more than being sorry for our sins. Repentance is seeing what it is possible for us to be and saying, "That's what I'm going to be. That's what God by His power is going to make of me." Repentance looks ahead as well as back.

Then you will notice that she is determined to get to Jesus. She broke every rule of etiquette. She broke all the rules of society. She crashed the party. She knew that they would throw her out, but she was determined to get to Jesus.

That reminds us of another woman who had a disease that the Bible calls an "issue of blood." They regarded that as ceremonially unclean. She was not allowed to go out into the company of other people. Yet she pushed through the crowd and touched the hem of Jesus, garment, breaking the customs and mores of her time in order that she might get to Jesus.

Zacchaeus, the tax collector at Jericho, climbed a sycamore tree in order to see Jesus. How undignified for a man in his position to do that! But he did it! He was determined to get to Jesus.

We need to have this same kind of determination. If you know anything about sports, you know that often the key to success is determination. In every area of sports you will find someone talented and gifted, but who lacks the will to win. You will find another with less talent who is determined to succeed and does.

Then we see in her an impulse to worship. Certainly, we need structured time to worship. We need places set aside to worship. We need to have a time to pray. We need to come to church at times of worship. We need to take the advantage that is offered to us in a sanctuary that is well-planned for worship, with beautiful music and beautiful surroundings.

But there also must be a spontaneous element to worship. There are times when you just feel like praying, when you feel like praising God. When you feel that impulse, you ought to respond to it.

Perhaps you are sitting at home and it comes into your mind to praise God. You may praise Him in your heart. Perhaps you are driving down the highway and you feel an impulse to pray. I suggest that on such occasions you should not close your eyes! You may not even want to pray or praise aloud, but in your heart you can respond to that impulse to worship.

If we may identify with the party-crasher in this scene, we may also identify with the guests. They were frustrated by the interruption.

A minister spoke once of how he planned his day carefully so that he could make the best possible use of his time. He wanted to do a good job. There were so many demands on his time. He planned his day very carefully. Then it was all spoiled by interruptions. Another, wiser minister said, "Those are not interruptions. They are unexpected opportunities." What the guests saw as an interruption, they should have seen as an unexpected opportunity.

Some of them, I'm sure, were totally indifferent to the woman who came in from the street. Their plan was to ignore her. "If you pay no attention to her, after a while she'll get discouraged and she'll leave us alone. Just pay no attention to her." That's a temptation that comes to us in life; to ignore people who need Christ, to ignore the cries of a needy world!

Others were ashamed. They wanted to put their best foot forward for Jesus. This was not the best representation of their city. This was not the kind of person they wanted to be in the welcoming party for Jesus. They were terribly embarrassed that she was there.

Some of them were angry. They didn't want to share Jesus with her. They wanted to monopolize His time and they wanted His undivided attention.

In their preteen years young people are often very possessive of their friends. They don't want their friend to be the friend of anybody else. That's their special friend. Teenagers outgrow that. But sometimes we really don't want to share Jesus with the world. We're troubled when visitors come in and take our favorite seat. We're troubled that great crowds come on special days and we can't get a convenient parking place. We really don't always want to share Jesus with those who need Him. We're angry when we must.

Undoubtedly there were some like Judas. He remarked on another occasion when a different woman had done a similar thing, "What a waste! That ointment ought to have been sold and the money given to the poor." Sometimes when one goes into a great church or cathedral, one hears that statement. "This beautiful house of worship should not have been built. The money should have been given to the poor." It's good to remember who said that first. It was Judas Iscariot.

No one believes in waste or needless extravagance. Yet one might feed the poor today and they will be hungry again tomorrow. Or one might build a great place of worship that nourishes the soul.

That surely is as important as nourishing the body. A great cathedral that will inspire men for a hundred years is not always a bad investment of God's money.

Certainly there were those who thought Jesus ought not waste His time on a woman like this. They thought she was hopeless and incorrigible. Once there was a scorpion who wanted to get across a river. He said to the turtle, "You're a very good swimmer. Let me hop up on the back of your shell and you can carry me across the river." The turtle said, "No, if I carry you across the river, you will sting me and I will die." The scorpion said to the turtle, "That's not logical. If I sting you and you die, I'll drown too." "All right," the turtle said, "You hop on the back of my shell and I will carry you across the river." But halfway

134

across the scorpion stung the turtle anyway and they both began to sink to the bottom. As they were drowning, the turtle said, "That wasn't logical. Why did you do that?" The scorpion said, "I guess it's just my nature."

Some people look at sinners and say, "That's just their nature. They won't change. They'll always be the same. They'll never be different." Jesus believed that people change.

So, we want to identify with Jesus, not with the woman who crashed the party and not with the guests in their varied reactions. Let us try to identify with Jesus. Jesus assumed the best motive.

I read this interesting statement: "Never attribute to malice that which can be adequately explained by stupidity." So many times we assume the worst motive.

Jesus had an advantage over us because He could read peoples' hearts. Yet He always looked for the best. He always assumed the best. It would have been possible to assume that this woman was coming in looking for customers. One might have assumed that she was making some kind of improper sexual advances to Jesus. There may have been those among the guests who assumed that. But Jesus always assumed the best motives.

You and I ought to do that. It is not naivete that calls us to do that. It is Christian love and charity.

Then Jesus saw the hidden potential! Nobody believed that this woman could ever amount to anything, but Jesus knew that she could.

For years astronomers talked about a dark hole in the sky. Their telescopes detected no light, no star, no planet in that great dark hole. They thought it was empty. Then the radio telescope was developed. When the radio telescope was trained on the dark hole in the sky, it began to receive signals; signals that indicated that there was something there. It was not really empty after all.

We look at lives and say they are empty. There is no virtue, there is no goodness there. There is no spark of the image of God left within them. But Jesus looks at those same people and sees what they can be. He knows that they have the potential to be great spiritual leaders. He turns sinners into saints and criminals into servants in His kingdom.

135

It is said that Thomas Edison had worked hour upon hour upon hour to perfect the world's first incandescent light bulb. Then he called his office boy upstairs to the workroom and said, "Now take this bulb downstairs. We will attach it to the electric current and we will have light." As the boy went down the stairs, Edison heard a crash. The world's only electric light bulb had been broken. So he set to work. After hours and hours of painstaking effort, he created the world's second incandescent light bulb. Then he called that same office boy. He said, "Take this bulb downstairs and when we have attached it to the current, we will have light."

I don't know if that story is true or not. It doesn't matter whether or not Thomas Alva Edison gave a boy a second chance. It does matter that God always gives us another chance, another opportunity. As long as there is breath within us, we have that opportunity. Jesus sees the hidden potential and reaches out to us because He wants us to reach that potential in life.

Stuart Hamblen was a down-on-his-luck singer in Hollywood. Because his career was not going well, he turned to drink and he became an alcoholic. He had almost wasted his life in alcoholism when Billy Graham came to Los Angeles for his great crusade. Stuart Hamblen went. He listened. He responded. He became a Christian. About a month later, a friend said to Stuart Hamblen, "Is it true that you have not had a drink for thirty days?" Stuart Hamblen said, "Yes, That's true. It's no secret what God can do." The friend said, "You ought to tell other people the story of what has happened. You ought to write a song about it." He did.

It is no secret what God can do.
What he's done for others, he'll do for you.
With arms wide open, he'll pardon you.
It is no secret what God can do.

Faith for Life's Mountains

If ye have faith as a grain of mustard seed, ye shall say unto this mountain, Remove hence to yonder place, and it shall remove: and nothing shall be impossible unto you.

(Matthew 17:20)

When Jesus spoke these words, He was standing at the northern extremity of Palestine at the foot of its highest mountain. Mt. Hermon towers 9000 feet above sea level. It is almost always mantled in snow. It's the tallest mountain in all the lands of the Bible. It was here that Jesus said, "If ye have faith as a grain of mustard seed, ye shall say unto this mountain, Remove hence to yonder place, and it shall remove."

This is a text that has always intrigued us. It is the kind of text where you like to let your imagination run. I can just picture myself as a mountain mover. Think how nice that would be. "Stand back folks, I'm going to pass off a miracle. You say I have no faith? Look at this. You want a demonstration of my faith? Let me show you something. See that mountain? I'm going to move that mountain to the other side of the river!" If I could do that, I would personally be the Greatest Show on Earth.

The interesting thing about faith is that it never lends itself to showmanship. Have you noticed that? All the things faith promises, true as they are, seem to melt away if we ever try to use our faith for showmanship.

If I let my imagination run in another direction, I can see myself putting out of business every bulldozer company on the face of the earth. "You want a new subdivision? Fine! Just call on me. I'll level all the hills and fill all the valleys. You want a new highway? You say you want it to run straight to its destination? No problem at all. I'll just move the mountains out of your way." I would be the richest man in the world if I were simply to go into the earth-moving business—the "Bob Shannon Faith Earth-Moving Business."

Here again we run into a little difficulty. Every time we try to turn faith into personal profit, it doesn't seem to work. Every time we try to turn faith to monetary advantage, to personal aggrandizement, it doesn't work. Jesus did not intend for His disciples to go into the earth-moving business. He did not intend for His disciples to go into show business. He is obviously not talking about moving literal mountains.

Jesus meant to say, "A little faith will accomplish a lot." He says so in striking and unforgettable language. If Jesus had simply said to us, "A little faith does a lot of good," who would have remembered that? Yet, this text was no surprise to you. You have remembered it across a lifetime as Jesus meant for you to. That's why He put it in this vivid and colorful language. Jesus is saying, "In your life you will discover that even a little bit of faith will accomplish large things."

There are some great things that need to be accomplished. In fact, if we want to, we may adopt Jesus' striking language. We may speak of mountains of guilt that need to be removed. That is, of course, not what Jesus was talking about. He was talking about this mountain, Mt. Hermon. Yet, we may use the same kind of language and speak of the large problems of life as mountains: mountains of doubt, mountains of fear, mountains of anxiety, mountains of regret, mountains of guilt that need to be moved—and that faith can move. So we sing, "Faith is the victory that overcomes the world."

That song is interesting because it is almost an exact quotation of Scripture. Jesus said, "This is the victory that overcomes the world, even our faith." That song is a very scriptural song. You will notice the song does not say, "Faith brings the victory," but, "Faith *is* the victory that overcomes the world."

Then I think of another song that I learned when I was a teenager in Christian service camp. We came back one time humming to ourselves the beautiful chorus—"God specializes in things thought impossible. He does the things that others cannot do." That's the heart of this text! God specializes in things thought impossible.

The word "mountain" in our text is not too hard to define. We can figure that out pretty well by ourselves. The difficulty in our text is in defining the word "faith." We all *know* what faith is. But we have a very hard time *saying* what faith is. Faith defies our definitions. We just can't quite put it into words. We know what it is and we know that we know what it is, but we find it hard to tell someone else what it is. It's far easier to say what it isn't.

Perhaps that's the best way to define faith. Some things come close to being faith, but fall short. Faith, for example, is not a guess. We guess about a lot of things. We guess about whether or not it is going to rain. We guess about the outcome of sporting events. We make a lot of guesses in life, but a guess is simply that. It is not based on facts. It has nothing behind it. One guess is as good as another. Faith is not a guess.

On the other hand, faith is not knowledge either. Sometimes when we express our faith in a very strong way, we say, "I know." Yet we realize that faith is not the same thing as knowledge. It lies somewhere between a guess and knowledge.

Nor is faith superstition. Christian faith is not the same thing as saying you believe in a rabbit's foot, a four-leaf clover, or a horseshoe nailed over your door. It is different from that. It is richer. It runs deeper. It has more behind it. It is not a guess, it is not knowledge, and it is not superstition.

Faith is not a universal intuition about God. That kind of thing exists. In his splendid books, *All Creatures Great and Small* and *All Things Bright and Beautiful,* the British veterinarian James Heriott describes the birth of a lamb. The grizzled farmer watched how unerringly the newborn lamb went directly to its mother's side. He shook his head and said, "It beats me how they know how to do that!" Animals have certain instincts.

Humans have certain instincts. Man has an instinct about God. Perhaps we should call it intuition.

Much has been said about women's intuition. Sometimes a woman will say to you, "I know something." You ask her, "How do you know that?" She'll say, "I don't know, but I know it." That's intuition—when you know something and you don't know how you know it, but you know it just the same.

There is a kind of universal intuition about God. I was talking with one of my neighbors once, a neighbor who never goes to church. She said, "Of course, I believe in a higher power. I think everybody knows there has to be a higher power." That's not Biblical faith. That's not Christian faith. If everybody knows it, what's distinctive about it? What's grand about it? This universal intuition, this thing that everybody knows about God, is not faith.

Nor is faith a kind of general optimism. Some people are quite sure that everything is going to turn out all right. They don't know how. They don't know who's going to make it turn out all right, but they're pretty sure that somehow life will work out. It may stem from the fact that they have excellent health or good digestion. Poor health will make you pessimistic and good health tends to make people optimistic.

This optimism may stem from a lot of good experiences they have had in life. In the past, life has pretty well sorted itself out in a rather nice way. They figure it's going to go on sorting itself out in the future.

Or it may be just a native characteristic, that has far more to do with the personality than it has to do with the soul. It is far more a matter of temperament than it is a spiritual thing. This general optimism is not faith.

Nor is faith a kind of brash self-confidence. "I can handle it. God and I can handle it, between the two of us." Such self-confidence is a very fine thing to have, but don't confuse it with faith.

Nor is faith a kind of reluctant persuasion. All the arguments are trotted out to prove God. Someone says, "You must be right. I certainly can't disagree with that. I guess you're right. There must be a God after all."

If a person is reluctantly persuaded ("Well, yes, I guess you must be right"), that is hardly faith. In the Bible faith is a joyful thing, an enthusiastic thing, a welcome thing. Faith is something that people reach out willingly to embrace, not something to which they are reluctantly dragged. The greatest arguments in the world will not convince the person who does not want to believe.

When we read the Bible we find some company in our difficulty in defining faith. As far as I know, there is only one definition of faith in the Bible. If there is any other, then I've missed it. It's in Hebrews 11:1. "Now faith is the substance of things hoped for, the evidence of things not seen."

That's a good definition of faith. It's an inspired definition of faith, therefore, we are certain that it is accurate. We are equally certain that it is not clear. "Faith is the substance of things hoped for, the evidence of things not seen." We'd like to focus it a little more clearly than that.

Apparently the writer of the book of Hebrews felt that the opening definition, accurate as it was, was not too clear. So he spent the whole rest of the chapter defining faith; defining it not in words, but in lives. The whole rest of that chapter is devoted to showing how faith worked in lives of various men and women. It is almost as if the writer said, "That's not clear enough for a lot of the people who are going to read this. It's got to be made clearer still. The way to make it clear is not to define it in words, but to describe it in the realities of life."

So, you read down through that chapter and find a fine definition of faith in terms of the lives that people live:

By faith Noah, being warned of God of things not seen as yet, moved with fear, prepared an ark.

By faith Abraham, when he was called ... went out, not knowing whither he went.

By faith Moses, when he was come to years, refused to be called the son of Pharaoh's daughter, choosing rather to suffer affliction with the people of God.

By faith they passed through the Red Sea as by dry land.

By faith the harlot Rahab ... received the spies with peace.

That's a representative sample of the rather long list in Hebrews 11. What things did all of these people have in common? There were a lot of differences. They were different people living in different places, under different circumstances. There must be some things they all had in common. If we can isolate those common denominators of faith, we will clearly see what faith is.

At least two common denominators of faith, were always present in every one of these lives that the Bible says was lived by faith. The first is written out plainly in Hebrews 11:8. We'll abbreviate the verse because it's a long complex sentence. "By faith Abraham went, not knowing." There's the first common denominator of faith—going not knowing.

The first characteristic seen in every one of these lives is that they lived by faith not knowing the future. Noah didn't know what the world would be like after the flood. He didn't even know how long it would rain, nor how long he would float in that little vessel until at last it would come to rest. So, Noah lived by faith because he lived not knowing the future.

Abraham went into a land he had never visited and yet he said he was going to make it his home. He had read no travel folders about the Holy Land. He had seen no slides from those who had been there. He had heard no description. He knew absolutely nothing about it. He went not knowing.

Moses did not know what lay ahead of him when he chose the people of God over the pleasures of Egypt. He didn't know that meant 40 years herding sheep in the wilderness. He didn't know that meant standing before Pharaoh demanding the release of his people. He didn't know that meant 40 years in the desert leading them to the land of Canaan. It was an unknown future that lay before Moses when he made his choice by faith.

The children of Israel did not know what lay ahead of them on the other side of the Red Sea, but they were going without knowing.

Rahab, the harlot who received the spies in Jericho, did not know what lay ahead for her. She knew only that there must be something better than the pagan gods of her people. There must be one, true, living, invisible God as these Jews believed. She didn't know if they would welcome an ex-prostitute or not. She didn't know if they would welcome an ex-pagan or not. She didn't know how a foreigner was going to get along living among those people. It was an unknown future that lay before her. That is the first common characteristic of faith—an unknown future.

The second is a known presence; a known God to whom one speaks, a God who listens, a God who will help; a God who will never desert those who put their trust in Him. Those are the characteristics of faith: an unknown future, a known presence.

There's one other word in our text that has to be considered and that's the word "seed." When we understand the mountain and the faith, all we have to do is understand the "seed."

"If ye have faith as a grain of mustard seed, ye shall say unto this mountain, 'remove hence to yonder place,' and it shall remove."

The mustard seed was the smallest of the seeds common to a farmer in Jesus' day. There are smaller seeds, of course, but among those commonly known to farmers at that time, there was none smaller than the mustard seed.

There's a good bit that we do not know about seeds. But there are some things that we do know.

The first is that every seed has an unseen power. You may feel that seed all you want to, but you will feel no pulse. You may put your stethoscope against it, but you will hear no heartbeat. You may cut it open, but you will see nothing that suggests life. But if you plant that seed, you will discover that it *has* life!

You will also discover that it has an enormous potential. The plant is always larger than the seed! This is universally true. There are no exceptions. In the world of nature, the plant is always larger than the seed. I have seen the mustard seed so tiny. I have seen the mustard plant taller than a man.

Jesus is telling us that a little faith will grow larger if it is cultivated. If we begin with just a little genuine faith, it will grow and grow and grow. We'll have a larger faith as days go by.

"The mustard plant," says Jesus, "grows large enough to shelter the birds of the air." There may be someone who wants to find shelter in your faith. There may be someone who has only a little faith himself and needs to take shelter in your larger, stronger faith. How many times have all of us, when our faith

143

was weak, turned to draw on someone else's faith! That's a common experience of life. That's the reason we cherish the friendships we have with great men and women of God. We know that when our faith is weak, theirs will be strong. Many times we have drawn upon the faith of a parent, wife, husband, minister, elder, teacher, or friend. It's a beautiful thing to have a faith large enough that someone else can take shelter in it.

Faith tells us that we have a future, too. Not only will our faith grow larger, but we, ourselves, will grow into a larger life.

There are two streets in Largo, Florida named Southview and Northview. There was not enough room on the map to write them out, so the mapmaker abbreviated. If you look on the map, you'll see So.view and No.view. I can imagine some stranger looking at the map, not seeing the little period after the abbreviation for north, and saying, "Now, there's a place I would not want to live: No View Street."

Faith never lives on such a street. Faith opens up for us a view of the eternal, a view of the future far better than the best of the present, far better than the happiest of the past.

Faith unleashes a potential, a power, in our own lives. The power of steam was available for a long, long time before it was ever harnessed and put to use. In 120 B.C. in Egypt they used the power of steam to turn a toy. Nobody ever thought of doing anything else with it for hundreds and hundreds of years until at last Fulton made his steamboat.

There were centuries between that little toy in Egypt and that steamboat, when all this power that could have been put to use had only been harnessed to playthings.

The power of faith is much too great to be put into playthings. It must, instead, be put to use on the meaningful issues of life; the hard realities of life.

Through it you can find forgiveness for sins and usefulness for life.

The Cup of Suffering

In Matthew 20:20-23 it is written:

Then the mother of Zebedee's sons came to Jesus with her sons and, kneeling down, asked a favor of him.

"What is it you want?" He asked.

She said, "Grant that one of these two sons of mine may sit at your right and the other at your left in your kingdom."

"You don't know what you are asking," Jesus said to them. "Can you drink the cup I am going to drink?"

"We can," they answered.

Jesus said to them, "You will indeed drink from my cup, but to sit at my right or left is not for me to grant. These places belong to those for whom they have been prepared by my Father" *(NIV)*.

"You will indeed drink from my cup"—the cup of suffering. In Gethsemane we identify with Jesus. We don't identify very closely with Jesus when He is healing the sick, walking on the water, or feeding the multitudes. We don't identify with Jesus teaching in the synagogue, cleansing the temple, or even hanging on His cross. We do identify with Jesus in the garden of

Gethsemane for each of us goes through his own private Gethsemane. Jesus prays, "Let this cup pass from me." That's our prayer too.

The cup of suffering is one all of us must taste. It is a part of life. It's inescapable. Our suffering may differ. For some people it is physical pain; hard, unrelenting, pain. For some people it is mental suffering. What decision will I make? Which road shall I take? For others it is the suffering we call heartache; that deep pain that goes to the innermost part of our being. The kind of suffering may differ, but every one of us must taste the cup of suffering.

We Americans suppose that happiness is our birthright. It may be that we came to that through a misreading of our Constitution. The Constitution of our country says that everyone of us is entitled to "life, liberty, and the *pursuit* of happiness." It never says we are entitled to catch up with it. Happiness is not our birthright. Suffering is our birthright. I don't want to be morbid or depressing about it, but I have to be honest and fair with you. Being born human makes suffering part of your birthright.

Job described it in chapter 14, verse 1. "Man that is born of a woman is few of days, and full of trouble." Sometimes when people suffer they do not recognize it as part of being human. They think that God is punishing them for something that they have done. That's a mistake. We know that is not true because of an experience that Jesus had.

Jesus came to a man born blind. His disciples asked Him, "Who sinned, this man or his parents, that he was born blind?" Now at first that sounds ridiculous. If he was born blind, how could it be in punishment for his sin? That was not an enlightened age like our own. In that day people believed in reincarnation. They believed that if you sinned in this life you were punished for it in a second life. So they said, "Who sinned, this man or his parents, that he was born blind?"

Jesus answered unequivocally, "Neither!" Jesus made it absolutely clear that the suffering we experience in life is not in punishment for our sins. It is rather a part of what it means to be human.

There is a verse we need to remember. It is Matthew 7:11. For some reason the numbers 7 and 11 seem to fit together. Maybe it's because they rhyme. But you can remember the number 7 and 11 and all you have to do is put Matthew in front of it.

"If ye then, being evil, know how to give good gifts unto your children, how much more shall your Father which is in heaven give good things to them that ask Him?"

God's gifts are good gifts. Always. If you got a bad gift, you may not know where it came from but I can assure you it did not come from God. All God's gifts are good gifts. James says, "Every good gift comes down from above, from the Father of lights." So to suffer merely means that you are part of the human family. If you want to avoid suffering you will have to resign from the human race.

Imagine that you are a football player. The minute that you put on the uniform you know that there is the possibility that you will suffer pain and maybe serious injury. But you go out on the field anyway. If you are hurt out on the gridiron you do not say, "Why me?" You knew when you put on the uniform that you would have to suffer to play football. So when we are born into the human family we come into a family of which suffering is always a part.

This cup, which all of us must taste, Jesus drained. He drank of it more fully than any of us ever can or ever will. You can see that in Gethsemane. "He sweat as it were great drops of blood." I don't know exactly what happened in the garden of Gethsemane. I don't know the physical explanation for that, but I know the meaning. Jesus' suffering was intense. It was intense because He suffered as man suffers and He suffered as God suffers. We do not ordinarily think of God suffering. That's because we fail to understand God. If you understand God, you know that God suffers.

He suffered as man suffers. He was nailed to a cross. These days when we execute a criminal we try to do it as quickly and as painlessly as possible. Society moved from the guillotine to the firing squad to the electric chair to the gas chamber and now to the lethal injection. We have reckoned that execution ought to be done as quickly and painlessly as possible. In Jesus' day it was just the opposite. They wanted it to last as long as possible and be as painful as possible. They invented crucifixion. Jesus died on the cross and suffered as man suffers.

But He also suffered as God suffers. For on the cross Jesus could look down into the future. He could see that some of the people for whom He was dying would be totally indifferent to His death. He could know that He was dying for people who would never care, for people who would make fun of His cross and spurn His sacrifice. That made His suffering all the worse. He suffered voluntarily. We don't do that. We shrink back from suffering. We try to avoid it whenever we can. Jesus walked into it with His eyes open and His head high. He said, "No man takes my life from me, I lay it down of myself." We have to be careful when we interpret that verse. We must not make it mean that Jesus committed suicide on the cross. It does not mean that. It does mean this. He had the power to stop it. He could have shrunk back from it. He could have refused it, but He let it happen. Voluntarily He went to the cross.

The Bible says He could have called legions of angels to rescue Him. Ray Overholt put this thought into a beautiful song.

He could have called ten thousand angels
To destroy the world and set Him free.
He could have called ten thousand angels,
But He died alone, for you and me.

He suffered voluntarily.

His suffering was undeserved.

I am choosing my words carefully here. *Some* of our suffering is deserved and *some* of our suffering is undeserved. Isn't that true? I would not be frank with you if I did not say that some of our suffering is deserved. Sometimes we suffer because of our sins, because of our thoughtlessness, because of our carelessness. Some of our suffering is deserved. Some of our suffering is undeserved. With Jesus it was different. All of His suffering was undeserved.

His suffering was vicarious. Have you ever wondered why preachers use words that you never hear in any other place? One reason is this. We have to discuss some very large ideas. There are some ideas so large that only large words can describe them. That is why when we come down to try to say that Jesus died in your place, we say it was vicarious.

148

Would you consider me irreverent if I said, "Jesus was our pinch hitter on the cross?" He took our place and experienced the suffering that we deserved.

When the Pope went to Warsaw, he made it a point to visit a jail cell in the city of Warsaw. It was a jail cell where a man had been imprisoned during the holocaust. That man was married. He had a wife. He had children. So a priest in Warsaw offered himself in exchange for the prisoner. He said, "I have no wife. I have no family. There are so many people depending on him. I offer myself in his place." The priest *was* put in that cell and the prisoner was released. The priest died there. He took the place of another man. Christ took the place of every one of us. "All the sin of the world on the Savior was hurled." He was the sin bearer for the whole human race. He suffered in our place. So the cup of suffering, a cup we all must taste, is a cup that Jesus drained.

The cup of suffering is also a cup that strengthens. Have you ever had the experience of buying a plant from a greenhouse, setting it out in the yard and watching it wilt and die? If you are going to take a plant from a greenhouse and set it outdoors, you have to do it gradually. That gradual process we call hardening. Suffering hardens us. It makes us strong.

In the days of the sailing vessels this is the way they chose a tree to make a mast. They did not go to some sheltered place where the trees were protected from the elements. They went up into the mountains where the soil was thin and rocky. They found a tree that had been buffeted by the storms and beaten by the winter winds. That tree, that hardened tree, they cut down for the mast of their ship. So suffering hardens and strengthens us.

A number of years ago I took a group on a trip to the Holy Land. It was a fairly strenuous journey. We had some late night events and some early morning departures. We had some long days. One lady in the group was a great deal older than the rest and I was worried about her. I was afraid she couldn't keep up the pace. But I noticed that she seemed to keep up the pace better than anybody else. Finally one day I said to her, "You're tough!" She said, "I have had a long time to get tough."

The sufferings of life toughen us. They help us to mature so that we are no longer spiritual children. Suffering makes us strong.

Have you ever watched a runner toward the end of a race? His face is distorted with pain. He has learned that if you do not run until it hurts, you never win. Suffering is necessary to victory.

Now the gain that comes to us though suffering may be described as a frozen asset. The equity in your home is a frozen asset. You cannot spend it to buy groceries or gasoline but it is an asset to you all the same. The good that comes to us from suffering may be described as a frozen asset. You can't spend it right now but it is going to be worth something to you sometime. As Paul said in 2 Corinthians 4: "For our light affliction, which is but for a moment, worketh for us a far more exceeding and eternal weight of glory."

Suffering teaches us. One of the things that it teaches us is courage. Sydney, Australia was first settled as a penal colony. Instead of putting people in jail in Britain, they shipped them off to Australia. Sydney was a great place for it because it is hemmed in by the mountains and the sea. When they had served out their sentence they were free to go, but there was no place to go. They didn't have enough money to come back to England. They were stuck in that little bowl that is now Sydney, Australia. They were pretty certain there was good land, but nobody was able to get to it. Many had tried and failed. They had gone up this valley and that valley and another valley. They would come back and say it was hopeless. So they called those mountains the Barrier Mountains. But two young men decided to try again. They decided not to try the easy way, going up the valleys. They decided to try it the hard way by attacking the mountain itself. They scaled it and found the land on the other side because they took the difficult route. Suffering teaches us courage.

Suffering teaches us the value of prayer. Suppose that prayer were nothing but thanksgiving and praise. Would prayer mean as much to you? Isn't it the fact that our prayers are wrought out in the white hot crucible of suffering that makes them valuable? We pray all night. We besiege God for something. Then we begin to see the value of prayer. And not just of prayer but of many other things as well. For when we suffer we come to see that some of the things we thought were worth a great deal are really worth very little. And we see some of the things that we thought were very little are truly worth a great deal.

Think a moment about Christ. Suppose the cross had never happened. Suppose Jesus had lived to be an old man, drifted into senility and died in His sleep. Would there then be any such thing as the Christian religion? You know the answer to that. It's "No." For Jesus took the cross and turned it into a hammer. He battered down the gates of Hell. He took the cross and turned it into a lever and moved the world. He took the cross and turned it into a bridge so that you and I might pass over from darkness to light and from death to life!

> I must needs go home by the way of the cross,
> There's no other way but this;
> I shall ne'er get sight of the Gates of Light
> If the way of the cross I miss.
> The way of the cross leads home,
> The way of the cross leads home,
> It is sweet to know as I onward go,
> The way of the cross leads home.
>
> (Jessie B. Pounds)

Spiritual Arsonists

Listen! Jesus is praying, praying in Gethsemane, praying under the shadow of the cross! He is praying for His disciples, He is praying for His church, He is praying for you!

> I pray not that thou shouldest take them out of the world, but that thou shouldest keep them from the evil. They are not of the world, even as I am not of the world. Sanctify them through thy truth: thy word is truth (John 17:15-17).

In these three brief verses, we can learn something about the church and something about the world.

First we learn that the church is in the world. Jesus said, "I pray not that thou shouldest take them out of the world." Many people do not realize that this is where the church belongs, in the world. There has always been the temptation to withdraw from the world. Sometimes the church has withdrawn from the world physically and gone behind great stone walls to hide away in monasteries, lest the church be smudged by the world. If you have ever traveled through Pennsylvania or through Ohio, you have seen another way of withdrawing from the world, not physically, but socially, economically, and practically.

Here you will see people driving buggies, dressed as their great-grandparents dressed; people who do not have television sets or radio sets; people who pay no attention to what goes on in the community, the nation, or the world. It is a monastery without walls. They have withdrawn from the world.

At a convention, one of the speakers was assigned a topic: "The Stained Glass Ghetto." Is that what the church is? A stained glass ghetto? Are we drawing apart behind the safety of stained glass windows? If that is the case, that is not what Christ intended. Christ wanted the church to be in the world. Some of you can remember a song once popular, "I don't want to set the world on fire, I just want to start a flame in your heart." Christians want to set the world on fire! That's the very purpose of their existence.

When there is a forest fire, sometimes the greatest protection is another fire. A man builds a little fire in a circle and when that burns off, he'll get inside the burned out circle. The fire he has built will protect him from the forest fire. So we want to set the world on fire for Jesus Christ, in order to protect the world from the fires of destruction that threaten it daily. Yes, we want to set the world on fire, and we want to do it by starting a flame of faith in every individual human heart. That's why Elton Trueblood entitled his book on the church, "The Incendiary Fellowship." That's why I'm calling this chapter, "Spiritual Arsonists." That's what we're out to do, to commit arson, to build fires in this old world that will protect us from the fires of Hell.

After the resurrection, our Lord walked with two along the road to Emmaus. They were prevented from recognizing Him, so that Jesus could have opportunity to explain to them the Scriptures. After He had done that and they got to their house, then they knew who Jesus was and He vanished. They said to one another, "Did not our heart burn within us, while he talked with us by the way, and while he opened to us the Scriptures? (Luke 24:32)." This is the way to set the world on fire for Jesus Christ: to open to them the Scriptures.

"Flaming hearts make flying feet." Those disciples whose hearts burned within them, raced back to Jerusalem to spread the good news that Christ was risen indeed. On the day of Pentecost, there appeared over the heads of the twelve apostles

154

tongues of fire. But the symbol was nothing compared to the substance. Those men had flaming tongues as they went first into Jerusalem and into Judea and then to the uttermost parts of the earth with the message that Christ was alive forevermore.

Yes, there are many examples to show us that God wants the church in the world because the only way you can start a fire is to put the flame where the fuel is. We can never set the world on fire by withdrawing from it but by rather getting into the middle of things. You can see that illustrated in the life of Jesus. Where do you find Jesus? You find Him going up and down the busy highways in Galilee. You find Him in the marketplace at Capernaum and at Jericho. You find Him on the streets in Jerusalem and in the temple. Wherever there crossed the crowded ways of life, wherever people were gathered, there you find Jesus in the midst: at a wedding feast in Cana of Galilee, in the synagogue on the Sabbath day, in the holy city on the feast days. Jesus was in the midst of things. This is where you find the apostles, and this is where you find the early church.

The Christians did not shun the forum, or the arenas, or the amphitheaters, or the modern life of their day. They moved among the people because that's where God wants the church to be. When the church gets out of its walls and into the community, then things happen.

The Bible also teaches us to view the church versus the world. "I pray not that thou shouldest take them out of the world, but that thou shouldest keep them from the evil" (John 17:15). There is a sense in which the church is set over against the world. While the church must always be in the world, the world must never be in the church.

A lot of people do not understand what it means for the world to get into the church. Some people think if we adopt a new style of music, that the world has gotten into the church. Others say that if you adopt a different form of architecture, you've brought the world into the church. There are some people who say that if we dress differently, or if we wear a different hair style than we did a few years ago, that the world has gotten into the church. None of these fits the description.

The world is in the church when sin gets in: jealousy, anger, lust, greed, dishonesty. That's what Christ wanted to prevent.

So He said, "I pray that thou shouldest keep them from the evil." It happens this way. The church becomes contented with the world as it is and no longer tries to change it. No longer is its heart broken by the world. Contentment is followed by compromise. The church says, "We have to give a little somewhere. Life after all is one big compromise. Everything in life is give and take." So the church begins to compromise with the world and yield to its standards.

Then at last there comes peaceful coexistence with the world. When that takes place, then the church has ceased to be the church. The church has a twofold task. One is that the church must continually call the world back to the moorings from which it has been loosed. The church must continually call the world back to principles now forgotten. It is also correct to say that the church is out ahead of the world, beckoning the world on. We're not resisting all kinds of change. We're only calling for change that is redemptive and renewing. The church calls to the world, saying, "Leave the dead life of the past and come with us into a bright and shining future." We have seen in this text that the church is in the world, but that it is also a case of the church versus the world.

Furthermore in this text we see the church serving the world. Jesus said, "Sanctify them." The word "sanctify" means to set apart for a holy use. Sanctification means sharpening the blade; putting the handle into the axe. People are not sanctified for the good it does them. We're sanctified in order to be of use to God and to others. It is the business of the church to serve the world.

There are two kinds of people, introverts and extroverts. The introvert turns inward and would rather read books or listen to music; the extrovert is more interested in other people. It doesn't make any difference which kind of person you are, but it does make a difference whether a church becomes an introvert or an extrovert. As long as the church is introverted, looking only at itself, at its inner life, at its mechanism, it will never get anywhere. The church must always be extroverted, looking out to hearts who are hungry and in need. Someone has said, that it is only in moving outside itself, that the church can truly be itself.

The church does not serve the world by being "Little Sir

Echo." That's been the case all too often. The church has waited to see which the wind is blowing and then set sail. The church has waited to see what public opinion is going to be and then jumped on the bandwagon. That's been the case with a lot of social changes that we are seeing. The church had nothing to say about them until they began to take place and then suddenly we hear churches and churchmen saying, "Me too! Me too!" The church does not serve the world by being "Little Sir Echo" to what the world is already saying. The church serves the world by saying, "Thus saith the Lord!"

Nor does the church properly serve the world by being the Lord's lobby in the courts of Caesar, by becoming a pressure group, another force to push people into this direction or into that. That's not the way the church is to serve the world. The church serves the world the same way fire serves man. Fire serves man by giving light. We know of no light that is not a result of fire—firelight, the light of the candle, the light in the incandescent bulb that comes from a little filament that is aflame, but like Moses' burning bush, almost never burns out. So the only spiritual light this world will ever know, will come from a church that is on fire with the truth of God. Then the light shines. We are to shine a light first of all upon the problem so that it can be clearly and properly understood. Then it is the church's job to shine the light of God's Word on the solution.

A wise man said, "No minister knows the solution to all the problems of the world, but every minister ought to know where to start." We start with the Word of God and the light it gives to men's lives.

Fire gives warmth. This is a cold and lonely world and people long for the warmth that can only truly be found in Christian friendship and in Christian fellowship.

Laski, who was not a Christian but a famous socialist, was discussing England during the days of the French Revolution. He said that England escaped the violence and bloodshed that France knew during that same period, even though England went through the same kind of changes. Then he said a surprising thing. He said the reason that England did not know the violence and bloodshed that France did was because of one man. He said it was because of the preaching of John Wesley.

John Wesley never discussed in his sermons one of those social evils. John Wesley called men back to God, and to their moral accountability before Him, but the result of it included great and sweeping changes in the life of a whole nation. That's the way the church serves the world.

The church loves the world. How can I reconcile that with the statement of Scripture that says, "love not the world, neither the things in the world"? I think both of them are looking at the same problem from different sides. God loved the world. "God so loved the world, that he gave his only begotten Son." The church must love the world—not sin, but men and women lost in sin.

Too often we are like the man who met an old acquaintance. He asked, "How's everything with you?"

The other man said, "Terrible. You know my wife just died."

The first man said, "Well, it could have been worse."

The other man said, "Not only that, but my son has been sent to jail."

The reply again was, "It could have been worse."

"Well," he said, "not only that, but I've just come from the doctor's office and he says I have an incurable disease."

Again, the man said, "Yes, but it could be worse."

By that time he'd had it. He said, "How in the world could it be any worse?"

The fellow said, "Well, it could have happened to me."

The church must never be that indifferent. The church must love the world and feel that the problems of this world are its problems too.

An old legend says that the apostle Thomas went to India. He was sold as a slave to the king of India and in this manner he was able to establish the church in India. And, so the legend goes, the king gave Thomas directions to build him a palace. Thomas would come to the king for money and then he would take the money and give it to the poor, or use it to spread the gospel.

The king asked, "When am I going to get to see my palace?"

Thomas said, "One of these days. One of these days."

Later the king asked, "How's my palace coming along?"

Thomas said, "Just fine, Just fine."

Finally, the king called Thomas in and said, "I do not believe you are building me a palace at all. When am I going to see my palace?"

Thomas said, "You will never see it in this life, but when you depart this life, you will see your palace, for it is built in the hearts of men."

It's only a legend, but what a lesson for life.

The Fox and the Lamb
(Luke 23:7-12)

DONE

DONE P. M. MAY 2 1999

In literature the fox has always stood for cunning and the lamb for innocence. In Aesop's fables it is the fox who guards the grapes he cannot eat. It is the fox who deceives and eats the gingerbread man. The expressions have become proverbial:

"Sly as a fox."

"I outfoxed him."

"The Prince," said Machiavelli, "must be a lion; but he must also know how to play the fox."

The fox stands for craftiness, cunning, and cruelty.

The lamb is always the symbol of gentleness and innocence. "Gentle as a lamb," we say. It was said of one that he was "a lion in the chase" but "a lamb at home." In the lodge ritual of a large fraternity the lamb is the badge of innocence. In the writings of Blake, the lamb is the badge of innocence.

The Bible describes Herod as a fox and Jesus as a lamb. The Pharisees had come to Jesus with a warning. "Herod is going to kill you." Jesus said, "Go tell that fox today and tomorrow I do cures and the third day I will be perfected." In other words, "I am keeping my schedule."

No man was more deserving of that title "fox." When his father, Herod the Great, died he left most of his territory to a younger brother and only little Galilee to Herod Antipas. He hurried to Rome to try to influence the emperor against his brother, but failed. Against another brother he was more successful. He seduced Herodias, his brother's wife. Eventually he shipped his first wife home and married Herodias. His sister-in-law became his wife, and she was already his niece. So the sin became a triple sin. It was that sin that John the Baptist fearlessly denounced. That was the reason Herodias demanded and got the prophet's head on a platter.

Nor was any man more deserving of the term "lamb" than Jesus. His introduction by John the Baptist contained just those words: "Behold the Lamb of God, who taketh away the sin of the world." Never was a man more gentle with children, with the sick, with the sinner. Never was a man so innocent. "He did no sin, neither was guile found in his mouth." When He challenged the crowd, "which one of you convicteth me of sin?" no one answered. Pilate's verdict is the only verdict. "I find no fault in him."

How perfectly He fulfilled Isaiah's prediction—"led as a sheep to the slaughter, and like a lamb dumb before his shearers." We must not suppose that His silence in our text was a deliberate fulfilling of the prophecy but rather that the prophet saw before what would, in fact, be the case.

Small wonder that in Revelation Jesus is pictured as the Lamb again and again. Small wonder that our songs reflect that thought so often.

"Dear dying Lamb, thy precious blood shall never lose its power."

"Are you washed in the blood of the Lamb?"

"Near the cross, O Lamb of God!"

In this text the fox and the lamb meet. Picture the scene. There sits Herod with all his soldiers arrayed behind him. How powerful he seems. How weak he is.

Jesus is standing alone. How weak He seems. How powerful He is. Herod has his bodyguards and all the palace crowd around him. Jesus is alone. Five thousand ate His loaves and fishes by the sea, but none of them are here now to defend Him. Twelve sturdy men had accompanied Him for more than three years, but none of them are here. He has friends in this place:

Nicodemus and Joseph of Arimathea. But they are not present to rise to His defense. If you were there and asked to join the winning side, you'd pick Herod at once. All the power of the Roman Empire is behind that puppet from Galilee. The carpenter seems a poor choice by comparison.

Yet the career of one ends in obscurity. The career of the other ends in grandeur. Indeed, if it had not been for Christ, most of us would never have heard of Herod. The fame of Christ has spread round the world and down the ages; and He is today the most powerful man of human history. Herod's life sputtered out in the obscurity of exile in France.

How quickly glory fades and power evaporates!

Yet we keep supposing that the answers to world problems lie with the Herods of the world and not with Jesus.

The world keeps betting on the fox and not on the Lamb. We ourselves often think that the odds favor the Herods of the world; that the odds lie with power, not with humility; that the odds lie with wealth, not with poverty; that the odds lie with cunning, not with innocence.

Once on a boat the disciples discovered that no one remembered to bring the picnic basket. There was only one loaf for all thirteen of them. Jesus said, "Beware of the leaven of Herod." They pondered that cryptic remark. Was He upset because there was no bread? What did He mean? He spoke it not only for them but for us. Jesus knew that through all time men would turn to Him for guidance. To us today, He says, "Beware of the leaven of Herod."

Beware of the sins of Herod. Lust and cruelty are in the world still. Beware of the idle and flippant curiosity, of Herod. Beware of the irreverence of Herod that makes men mock holy things.

Beware of the tendency to talk when silence would be better. If Herod had only known the true situation, he would have kept silent. If he had known that he was in the presence of the King of kings, would he have dared to demand a miracle? Would he have dared to play the little game of masquerade? Would he have dared to mock and ridicule?

King Henry went to hear Latimer preach. The great man began by giving himself some public advice: "Latimer," he said, "be careful what you say. The king of England is here." He added, "Latimer, be careful what you say. The King of kings is here."

In this text the fox and the lamb meet. And it is the fox who is afraid.

Verse 8 hints at this and Luke 9:7-9 makes it plain. Herod had never really gotten over the execution of John the Baptist. No doubt he secretly admired the man. He had spoken rashly at the birthday party, promising the seductive Salome anything she wished. When the request was for the head of John, Herod was, says the Bible, exceedingly sorry. Herod never forgot how weak he had been, how he had been manipulated, how cruel he had been.

When Jesus came along, so like John, curiosity arose in the heart of Herod—and turned to fear. What if John had indeed come back from the dead! What if he was only biding his time for vengeance? How sin makes men afraid!

Jesus' silence seems fitting. He would not remove from Herod that fruit of sin he so fully deserved. Let him wonder. Let the anxiety smolder.

Jesus is remembering how desperately John had sent word from prison to find reassurance that his life had not, after all, been in vain. And the cruel and needless execution of that great preacher must have surely filled His heart with strong emotion. He may have kept silent because He dared not speak. So strong was that emotion, He may not have trusted himself to say anything. To speak would calm Herod's fears. Silence only makes them grow deeper.

Herod's fear is also mixed with a certain curiosity. Again look at verse 8. Everybody likes to see a magician perform his tricks. Many like to believe there is something supernatural about it. It amazes us how willing, how anxious people are to believe in magic.

The reports that have come to Herod about Jesus are exciting. He wants to see those miracles of healing. But how would that look! Imagine, the governor of Galilee going out to some hillside to watch a carpenter teaching and healing! Of course, his position would not let him do that. But now he has a chance at last to satisfy his coarse curiosity about Jesus, and Jesus properly will not honor it.

We may sometimes come to the Bible with such an unholy attitude. The Bible is far, far more than an old curiosity shop. If all you are interested in is viewing its curiosities, then stay away. We must come here as Moses did before the burning bush, without our shoes, recognizing that this is holy ground.

Men do strange things when they are afraid and frustrated. Some whistle. Others laugh. Herod is in the second category. Verse 11 says that he "set him at nought." That is translated by some as "made light of him" or "treated him with contempt." They ridiculed Him, made fun of Him, and mocked Him. They put on Him a gorgeous robe. He could have struggled against the ugly charade, tried to shake off the robe, cried out, "Stop it!" But Jesus never lost His dignity. He bent to receive that robe with all the grace and bearing of a king. Never in His life had He worn anything half so fine as that. How odd it looked over His rough Galilean garments. Yet never a man deserved to wear it more than He.

In the story of the crucifixion people kept unknowingly doing appropriate things. Judas betrayed with a kiss. Did not Jesus deserve the loving kisses of the world? The soldiers gave Him a reed for a sceptre! Never did a man deserve more to hold the sceptre of power! Pilate put up a title: King. He put it in three languages so that no one would miss the joke. What is more appropriate than that the Lord of all mankind should be identified trilingually?

So here, though the scenes make our blood run cold, there is a cruel appropriateness to it all. Herod and his soldiers play their little game of charades. Does he hope to provoke Jesus to speech? Is he bored with palace routine? Is it some devilish streak in his nature that prompts such action? We cannot know. We recoil from the scene. Herod and his men soon tire of it. In the gorgeous robe, Jesus is sent again to Pilate.

But let us not miss the importance of verses 9 and 10. The tendency when one is accused is to answer back—quickly, firmly, at length. Why does Jesus offer no defense? Perhaps it is because some charges ought not to be dignified with a defense. Years ago, when everybody was hunting Communists, it was not hard to find pages of accusations hurled at high public officials. Often they were silent in the face of such slanders. I wondered why. I even sometimes naively thought that their silence proved their guilt. I am older now. I know what Jesus obviously knew all along. One does not dignify every charge against Him with an answer. Some accusations are not worthy of an answer.

So, as charge after charge is hurled against Jesus, He stands calm and unruffled in dignified silence. We admire Him far more for that than if He had shouted, "Lies! Lies! They're all lies! You made that up!" True enough that would have been. But Jesus would have lost something of dignity and honor and manhood. And looking at the scene today, we know He did exactly right. He ignored those clamoring voices as if they were no more than wind in the trees.

Thus went the first meeting between the fox and the Lamb. It was not the last. Herod and Jesus met again. This time Herod was the prisoner in the dock. This time Jesus was the judge. This time it was Herod who was speechless!

Reprinted from PULPIT DIGEST, January/February, 1982. Used by permission.

The Hawk
and the Dove

In Matthew 27:15-18, 20 is the following story:

Now it was the governor's custom at the Feast to release a prisoner chosen by the crowd. At that time they had a notorious prisoner, called Barabbas. So when the crowd had gathered, Pilate asked them, "Which one do you want me to release for you: Barabbas, or Jesus who is called Christ?" For he knew it was out of envy they had handed Jesus over to him.
But the chief priests and the elders persuaded the crowd to ask for Barabbas and to have Jesus executed (NIV).

Barabbas was a small-time criminal. He had organized a little band of revolutionaries, but he was not motivated by any real patriotic fervor. He only used patriotism as a cloak to hide his schemes to rob and steal. If somebody got in the way and got killed, well, it was just too bad for them.
So, Barabbas and two of his followers eventually were caught, tried and sentenced to be executed. Try to imagine how Barabbas felt. He is lying in a dark prison cell. He knows that he is going to be put to death. Every day he thinks about his execution.

Then all too soon, he hears the sound of footsteps coming down the corridor. The door to his cell is thrown open. "All right, Barabbas. Let's go." As he leaves the cell, he hears shouting from the streets above. "Crucify him! Crucify him!" He cannot imagine that people hate him so. But that's what they're shouting—"Crucify him!" He hears his own name. "Barabbas, Barabbas." He is astonished to be the object of such anger.

Then they lead him blinking out into the bright sunlight to stand beside a total stranger before the crowd. Then the crowd suddenly cries for Barabbas to be released and for this other man to be crucified!

To his astonishment, Barabbas is free. He has been programming his mind for his execution. Now, suddenly, he is free! He doesn't know what to do! Perhaps he wanders the streets in some kind of a daze while his two associates and that other man are led away to be crucified.

We really don't know much about Barabbas. In fact, we don't even know his name. For Barabbas is not a name. "Bar" in the Bible always means "son of." Barabbas means "the son of Abbas." And it may be that that was, in fact, his father's name. But "abbas" means "father." So, his name in the Bible, "Son of the father" may have been a nickname. Many think that's the case. At any rate, we do not know his name.

But one obscure manuscript does give us a name for Barabbas. If it may be believed, that manuscript says that Barabbas had the same name as our Lord. That when those two people stood before the crowd, there was Jesus of Nazareth and there was Jesus Barabbas.

That's possible because the name Jesus was a common name at that time. It was as common as John, Bob, or Bill are today. Jesus was only a form of the name Joshua. Many a parent named a child for that great hero of the Old Testament, Joshua. And it is possible that that was Barabbas' name. In Latin countries you will still find people named Jesus.

But whether his name was that or something else, only one thing is certain—he exchanged places with our Lord. Are you surprised that the crowd chose Barabbas instead of Christ? Are you surprised that they chose the taker of life instead of the giver of life, that they chose the robber instead of the giver, that

168

they chose the man of war instead of the man of peace, that they chose the sinful man instead of the innocent man? Does that surprise you?

It ought not. The world continually chooses Barabbas instead of Jesus. The world continually opts for power before principle, for force rather than nonviolence, for war rather than peace, for taking rather than giving.

Now we think that we would have picked the good man. We always want the honest man, the man of integrity. But do we really want that? For example, suppose you are in serious trouble and you need a lawyer. Do you want an honest lawyer?

A preacher talked to a man one time who had some problems. The preacher said, "I know a good man who is a lawyer." The man replied, "I don't want a good lawyer, I want the crookedest lawyer in town."

We might not all be that frank about it, but do you want an absolutely 100% honest, straight-arrow man for your lawyer? Do you want a 100% honest, straight-arrow man for your accountant? Do you want a 100% honest, straight-arrow man for your friend? You may sometimes want your friend to lie for you or to cover for you. We too sometimes pick Barabbas instead of Jesus.

The plot of the story is that they exchanged places: Barabbas and Jesus. That's a plot that you see sometimes in literature and life.

Maybe you read the story *The Prince and the Pauper.* It's the story of two little boys. One was the child of the king and one was a child of the streets. They exchanged clothing and they exchanged identity. The little boy from the slums went to the palace to live with the king. The little boy who was the king's son went down into the slums to live in a hovel.

This exchanging of places sometimes happens in real life. The newspaper told of two sisters who very much resembled one another. One of the them was found guilty of a crime and sentenced to jail. She had a family. Her sister had no children. So, when the day came for her to begin serving her sentence, the sister came in her place. Nobody bothered to check the fingerprints. For a year the innocent sister was in jail and the guilty sister was free.

Here in the story of Barabbas and Jesus we have a similar thing. For Barabbas there was no choice. Jesus did have a choice. He chose to take Barabbas' place and our place. We deserved to die on that cross. The wages of sin is death and We've sinned, but He took our place. He took our place literally. He took our place legally. He took our place spiritually. Just as He took Barabbas' place, He took our place.

Let's think about Barabbas, particularly on that Saturday after the crucifixion and before the resurrection. We know where Jesus was. He was dead and buried. Where do you suppose Barabbas was? What do you suppose he was doing? Don't you think he celebrated a little? Maybe he celebrated a lot. Maybe he found some of his old friends and said, "I don't understand it, but something wonderful has happened and I'm free. I'm not going to die. I'm going to live."

But maybe on Saturday night when the celebration was over, Barabbas started to think about what had happened to him, Maybe he started to think about that "other man" who now was dead.

Suppose that you have committed a serious crime. Someone else is arrested, charged with your crime, found guilty and sentenced to die. How would you feel? Every day you would open the newspaper and there would be the story of efforts that people were making to spare him from the electric chair. And all the time you would know that he is innocent and that you are guilty.

Then one day you'd open the paper and read that the sentence had been carried out. He's dead and you're alive. You committed the crime and he was innocent. How would you feel?

We have a little taste of it in this country. It is no secret that we are free in this country because somebody died to make it possible. The name Nathan Hale comes to mind. He died for American freedom. But, of course, there were thousands.

The battlefield of Blue Licks is where the last battle of the American Revolution was fought. It was a battle that never should have been fought. It was a battle that was fought when the war was over. We had already won the war for American independence. The news had not yet reached the frontier. There, in Kentucky and West Virginia, the battle still went on.

There is a stone at the battlefield of Blue Licks with the names of the men who died in the battle. In that list of names was the name Robert Shannon. One of my ancestors died in the Battle of Blue Licks for my freedom. That makes it a little more touching to me.

All of us need to focus sharply when we think about someone who has died for our freedom. To speak of thousands doesn't move us nearly as much as to focus on a single individual or two. Perhaps many of us can do that.

For me it has always been Bobby True. He was the same age as my sister. He was a genial, affable, gay-hearted young man who went off to fight in France and died before the age of eighteen for my freedom.

I also think of Gene Martin who was my age. We went to school together. He went to Korea and died on Pork Chop Hill. If I can focus on these individuals, then I can appreciate a little more what it means that somebody died so that I can be free.

We focus on a person. We focus on a place. That's why we have Independence Hall in Philadelphia, Pennsylvania. People go there and take their children there. They say, "This is where it happened. This is where our freedom began."

In England they don't go to a building, they go to an empty field, Runnymede, where King John was forced to sign the Magna Carta. The Swiss go out to an empty field. Rutli Meadow was where the Swiss Confederation was born. The Irish go to a jail! Of all the shrines of national liberty in the world, none is more striking than that. They go to a jail in Dublin. There on a sunny Sunday morning a group of Irish patriots were led out into the courtyard and executed. That's the focus of their political freedom in Ireland.

With regard to our spiritual freedom, can we not focus just that tightly on a certain place—Golgotha? On a certain person—Christ? Without Him and what He did there, we could never be free from guilt, never be free from the burden of sin, never be free from the power of sin! This is where our spiritual freedom began.

In Grant county, Kentucky, there was an unusual tourist attraction. Along the highway someone had set up the last gallows on which anyone had been hung in the state of Kentucky.

People would stop and gawk at that gallows. Suppose that you know absolutely nothing about the Christian religion. It is all totally new to you and you walk into church some Sunday morning and they start talking about a cross. A cross is no different than a gallows or an electric chair. What a strange symbol for our religion! Can you imagine people going around with a little gold gallows on a chain? Or a little gold electric chair on the lapel? That's just how strange it would seem to you if you were hearing it for the first time. We've heard it so often that we miss the impact of it.

The fact is that the cross was the key that unlocked the chains that bound us to sin. The cross set us free and there is nothing like that freedom.

Skydivers say that it is a marvelous feeling of freedom to step out of an airplane into the sky and just float there for a while.

Glider pilots say that when the tow plane cuts them loose and they fly free, soaring like a bird, silently through the air, it is a great sense of freedom.

The longing to be free is something that is deep within us. But the greatest freedom we need is the freedom from sin, the freedom from guilt, the freedom from the powers of darkness. It is accomplished for us in the death of Christ and only in the death of Christ. Not only do we find our freedom there, we find our life there.

Suppose that you have a serious kidney ailment. You must have a kidney transplant. Some close relative of yours volunteers to donate a kidney to you. Then you learn that he has only one and has offered to donate it to you. How would you feel?

It may be that your mother died giving you birth. If that's the case, how did you feel when you first heard about it?

Edwin T. Dahlberg was a celebrated Baptist minister in St. Louis, Missouri. He said that he had an older brother who had the same name as he—a brother who died in infancy. He said that when the baby died his mother was inconsolable in her grief until she learned that she would have another child. So, when he was born they gave him the same name as the child that had not survived. He said that all of his life he had heard about Edwin that lived and Edwin that died.

He said that he'd stood in the cemetery and looked at the

tombstone that had his name on it—Edwin T. Dahlberg. He said, "I never stood there without the feeling (once definitely confirmed to me by my mother) that if he had not died, I would never have lived."

We all have such an elder brother. We wear His name. We live in the certain knowledge that if He had not died, we could never have lived.

The Robber and the Redeemer
(Luke 22:1-6)

For a long time Judas had been taking money from the meager funds of Jesus and the twelve. When his eyes met the eyes of Jesus, Judas realized that Jesus knew. Something had to be done. He hit upon a plan that would eliminate the one person who could testify against him, give him a new direction in life, and make a little money in the deal.

Having conspired with Jesus' enemies, he then looked for a convenient time and place to hand Jesus over to them. The opportunity came in the garden of Gethsemane. Jesus had been praying. Suddenly the officers arrived. Judas was in the midst. He stepped forward to kiss Jesus. It was the customary greeting of that time. It was no more unusual then than a handshake is today. But here the kiss is the signal. As the officers moved in to arrest Jesus He said to Judas, "Do you betray the Son of Man with a kiss?"

Judas will always remain a mysterious figure. We try to figure him out and cannot. There are three views about Judas. One is the charitable view. This view is held by those who say that Judas wanted to force Jesus' hand. He had seen the miracles. If he could get Jesus to turn those miracles against His enemies, great things could be done. He wanted to force Jesus to use His

.aculous powers to destroy His enemies and establish His ingdom.

That's the charitable view. I do not subscribe to that view. It is theologically unsound. But I am glad that there are people who hold that view. I am glad that there are people who want to put the best face on everything. The world has enough people who want to construe everything in the worst possible way. I am glad there are a few who try to construe everything in the best possible way. People like that I take for my models in living, but not for my teachers in theology.

The second view is the demonic view. This is the view that Judas was not really a person like us, but a demon in human form. They say he was created for the very purpose of betraying Jesus. There are three things wrong with that view. First, there are really not many prophecies about Judas. The ones we have are very sketchy. It's always a mistake to say that events took place in order to fulfill prophecy. Just the opposite is the case. Prophecies were given because events were going to take place. This view makes God the betrayer of Jesus, and I don't like that. The view is based on that Scripture verse in which Jesus says, "I have chosen you and one of you is a devil." But Jesus also said to Peter, "Get thee behind me, Satan." It means the same in both instances. We cannot accept the demonic view.

The third view is the common view, that Judas started out well enough and then changed. He began to steal from the common treasury. He began to suspect that he was going to be found out and exposed. He knew that Jesus knew. Gradually his love turned to hate. There are many kinds of hatred in the world, but the most bitter is that which grows in the soil of love. Love turned inside out, love turned into hate, is the most bitter hatred of all. That's what happened to Judas. He began by loving Christ. He ended by hating Christ.

We can identify with Christ in this story because we all have sometimes felt betrayed. It is a common experience of life to trust someone and then have them betray that trust. Perhaps you've been betrayed by a marriage partner, or by a business partner, or by a friend, or by someone in your family. But it is a common experience, and one man put it in a little verse:

I want men to remember me
When grey death sets me free.
I was a man who had many friends
And many friends had me.

When you feel that someone has "had" you then you begin to
identify with Christ.

The word "traitor" is an ugly word in any language. During
the American War of Independence there was a captain in the
Connecticut militia. He was soon promoted to colonel and then
to brigadier general and then to major general. He fought
bravely in battles against the British at Ticonderoga, Lake Cham-
plain, and Saratoga. Twice he was seriously wounded. Congress passed a special resolution commending him for his hero-
ism and thanking him for the contribution to American
independence. He name was Benedict Arnold. He is remembered not for any of those things. He is remembered because he
changed sides and became the most famous traitor of the American Revolution.

We have seen the country betrayed, the cause of Christ betrayed, and sometimes we have felt that we have personally
been betrayed. We identify with Christ in His betrayal. We do
not identify with Him in our response to betrayal.

Christ did not allow that betrayal to make Him angry or bitter.
He didn't allow it to tempt Him to give up. He didn't say,
"They're all like that!" Many a wife has counseled with the
minister about her own experience of betrayal and said, "I hate
all men! I could never trust another man!" Jesus didn't do that.

He didn't fight back or try to get even. We may identify with
Him at the point of betrayal but not at the point of response to
betrayal.

Some of us may identify with Christ in this story, but all of us
identify with Judas. When Jesus was in the upper room with the
disciples He said, "One of you betrays me."

No one said, "Is it Judas?" Everyone said, "Is it I?"

And that's what we say — "Lord, is it I?" For we all feel that at
some point in life we have betrayed Christ. We didn't intend to.
We didn't want to, but we did. None of us planned to fail Him,
but we did. And like Judas, it did not come suddenly.

We began to make little compromises. They grew and grew. Perhaps, like Judas, ours began with greed. How dangerous that disease is! Perhaps, like Judas, ours began with ambition, unbridled ambition, ruthless ambition. We cast ourselves in the role of Judas. It has been said that there is a little larceny in us all. It has been said that every man has his price. I hope it isn't so, but it's been said.

Certainly everyone is sometimes tempted to steal. It may be only keeping the change when someone gave you too much. It may be defrauding the government by cheating on your income tax. It may be a large sum, it may be a small sum, but we are all tempted to be dishonest. The first dishonest step may be only a small one, but it makes it easier to take another and another and another; each one larger than before.

When people *are* strictly honest it's news. The newspapers in Tampa, Florida carried the story of two little boys who found a paper sack with more money in it than any two little boys ever expected to see. They returned it to its owner and it made the news. I'm glad it was in the newspapers, but I'm sad that it was considered sensational. I wish the article could have said, "As expected, they returned the money!"

Other newspapers carried the story of Dwayne Morgan of Santa Ana, California. He had been laid off from the aerospace industry. He was unemployed and almost broke. He sat down on a park bench and saw lying beside him a tattered wallet. Inside it was five thousand dollars. He turned it in and the story made the news. An executive at Douglas Aircraft in Long Beach read about it, and gave that man a job.

We've always been told that honesty is the best policy. But we must determine to be honest, whether or not it is the best policy. Even if it does not work to our advantage; even if it works decidedly to our disadvantage, we must be honest.

We can further identify with this story when the Bible writes for us Judas' obituary. It says, "He went to his own place." We know that he went back to the chief priests and returned the thirty pieces of silver. We know that he hanged himself. And after that, "He went to his own place." He went to the place for which he was prepared.

Many people don't like to go to church. They don't like the

songs, the sermons, the prayers, the fellowship. If you forced those people to spend eternity listening to that music it wouldn't be Heaven for them. So they go to their own place; to the place for which they are prepared.

A lady described once her brief venture into the world. She went to a cocktail lounge at that hour that is foolishly and inaccurately called "the happy hour." She didn't see very many happy people there. She looked around and said, "I don't belong here. This is not my crowd. These are not my kind of folks." It was not her place, and she left.

When we die we go to our own place. Judas went to his own place. And Jesus? He went to His own place: Heaven.

In 1649 King Charles I of England was brought to trial for high treason. The sentence was, "He deserves to die." Four noblemen rose from the crowd and offered themselves to die in his place. But the offer was refused. They said, "He deserves to die."

We read about Judas and we say, "He deserves to die." Then we think about it for a while and we change that sentence ever so slightly. We say, "We deserve to die." Then Jesus stands up in the courtroom of the soul and says, "I will die in their place." It is a mark of the love and grace of God that He permits the substitution to take place.

Two missionaries once came to a primitive society. They were not at all successful. They could make no headway. But while they were there a strange thing happened. Two young men got into an argument. The argument turned violent. One killed the other. Then, according to the inflexible code of that society, he had to give himself up to the father of the murdered man. Everyone knew what to expect, and so did the murderer. But he went. He said, "I have killed your only son and now I surrender myself to you." The old man sat thoughtfully for a while. Then he said, "Now I have no son. So you will be my son. And when I die you will inherit all that is mine." His punishment became his salvation!

When the villagers heard about it, they all gathered at the missionaries' hut. They said, "Now we understand what you have been teaching us."

Amazing grace! How sweet the sound,
That saved a wretch like me!
I once was lost, but now am found,
Was blind, but now I see.

(John Newton)

One Day in the Life of the Governor
(Matthew 27:19-26)

All that we know of Pontius Pilate is this one day in his life, one page from Jewish history, and two stones with his name on them. We judge Pilate by day out of his life. If I judged you by one day out of your life, you'd cry, "Foul!" You'd say that it's not fair. Some days we are better than others. Is it fair to judge Pilate by one day out of his life?

If it were one day selected at random, it *would* be unfair. But some days are so crucial that they are a fair basis to judge an individual. There are days of great opportunity and great temptation. Sometimes a single day is a window into the very soul of a man. This day was such a day. We can see Pilate's attitude toward Christ, his attitude toward himself, and his attitude toward the future. If you know that about a man you know a lot.

The ultimate judging of humanity is based on one's attitude toward Christ. When Pilate asked "What shall I do with Jesus?" he asked a crucial question. His answer to it is instructive. Your answer to that question is also instructive.

Much about Pilate is positive. Of the four rulers before whom Jesus was tried that night, only Pilate treated Him with respect; only Pilate showed any pity or any tenderness. That was not true of Caiaphas, Annas, or Herod. Pilate treated Jesus differently and he deserves to be given credit for it.

Also, if you study all these trials, you will discover that Jesus had only one witness for the defense, and that was Pilate. Pilate and Pilate alone testified in His favor. Pilate did ten positive things to help Jesus avoid execution. He permitted Him to speak for himself. He examined Him privately, away from His accusers. He sent Him to Herod to avoid the problem. He said, "I find no fault in Him." He said, "Herod finds no fault in Him." He said, "He is a just man." He said, "Behold the man!" He made a real attempt to release Jesus. When that failed he tried to substitute Barabbas. When that failed he had Jesus whipped. He thought that would induce pity and the crowd would no longer demand His execution.

Yet when all of that was done, Pilate had Him crucified. Why? It was not out of friendship for the Jews who demanded Jesus' death. Roman governors had been sensitive to Jewish feelings. The Romans carried on their flagstaff an eagle, symbol of the emperor. They said that that emperor was divine. That offended the Jews because they said it was an idol. Those before Pilate had taken it off when the troops marched into Jerusalem. Pilate said, "No! Leave it on the standard!" It offended the Jews.

When he wanted to build an aqueduct and put in a city water system, he took money from the temple treasury to pay for it. That enraged the Jews. They hated Pilate. Pilate responded in kind. He didn't do it out of friendship for the Jews.

He didn't do it because he believed the charge of treason they brought against Jesus. Nor was it that Pilate cared for the charge of blasphemy they raised against Jesus. Why then did Pilate crucify Jesus, whom he had so vigorously defended?

The answer lies in a decision Pilate had made a long time before. He had decided that his life would be ruled by one thing: ambition. He resolved that nothing and nobody was going to stand in the way of his progress. Having made that decision long before, now on the basis of it he sent Jesus to be crucified. While we are puzzling over that, let us recall that we, like Pilate, have said some very nice things about Jesus and then crucified Him. The Bible says that when we Christians sin we crucify Jesus afresh.

What was Pilate's attitude toward himself? What was Pilate's verdict on Pilate? "I am innocent," he said. Only a few have ever believed him. In Africa the Abyssinian church said that Pilate became a Christian. They made him a saint. In Egypt the Coptic church said that not only did he become a Christian, but that he died for his faith. They made him a martyr. Most of the Christian world has not agreed with that opinion. Scripture certainly does not picture Pilate as innocent. The apostle's creed is the oldest creed in Christendom. It does not picture Pilate as innocent. Jewish history, written by Josephus, does not picture Pilate as innocent.

No, here is a man who had convictions but no courage. If we fear a man without convictions, we ought to fear equally the man with convictions who lacks the courage to carry them out.

Pilate is like many others when he delivered this verdict on himself. "I am innocent," he said. That's what Adam and Eve said in the garden of Eden. That's what every arrested criminal says.

I knew of a county sheriff who had transported many to the state prison. He said that he never took a man to state prison who did not claim to be innocent.

"Society is to blame!" people say.

"My parents are to blame!" people say.

"My Irish temper is to blame."

"The schools are to blame."

"The churches are to blame."

"My psychiatrist is to blame!" (Recently a man sued his psychiatrist because his psychiatrist didn't prevent him from committing a crime!)

Often we hear a person pronounce this verdict on himself: "I am innocent." But it is something you will never hear a Christian say!

When my Catholic neighbor went to confession he used to say in Latin, *"Mea Culpa*—I am to blame." And that's right. Once I appeared on a panel with a rabbi. He kept talking about Christians blaming the Jews for the crucifixion. I said to him, "I've been in the church all my life and I was *never* taught that the Jews were to blame for the crucifixion of Jesus. I was taught that I was to blame."

183

In the upper room when Jesus gave us the Lord's supper He said, "One of you will betray me." Each of the twelve asked, "Lord, is it I?" Ever since, Christians coming about the Lord's table have said the same words, but in a different order. For those first disciples it was a question. For us, it is a confession. They asked, "Lord, is it I?" We say, "Lord, it *is* I."

Then we see Pilate's attitude toward the future. Pilate was a man who lived for today. We are constantly being urged to do that. And up to a point that's all right. There is a point beyond which that's all wrong. The person who lives *only* for today will never slave to get an education. The person who lives *only* for today will never save for retirement. The person who lives *only* for today will never prepare for the judgment. And *that* lay in Pilate's future!

All that we know of Pilate comes from this story in the Bible, those two stones, one page in history, and a legend. History says that there was an uprising in Jerusalem. Pilate quelled it with excessive force and the Jews complained to Rome. He was summoned to Rome to appear before the emperor, Tiberius, but on his way the emperor died. He never did have to account for his deeds. In Rome he was caught up in the bureaucratic shuffle and posted to some insignificant part of the empire. Here he disappears from history.

But legend takes up where history leaves off. Legend says that when Pilate died they threw his body into the Tiber River. Such a storm erupted that they had to fish it out. Then they threw his body into the Rhone River. Such a storm erupted that they had to fish it out. Then they threw it into the lake of Lucerne, where it remains to this day. And the mountain that rises above Lucerne is still called Mt. Pilatus. But that's all legend!

It *is* true, though, that he was summoned to Rome to appear before the emperor. It *is* true that the emperor died before he got there, and Pilate did not have to stand trial before Caesar. He did, of course, stand trial. He stood trial in a higher court than Caesar's; in the highest court of all. This time Jesus was the judge and Pilate the prisoner in the dock.

The Bible assures us that Jesus is indeed the judge of all people. Acts 10:42 says that He has been appointed judge of the living and the dead. Acts 17:31 says that God has appointed a day in which He will judge the world by that man whom He has ordained. John 5:22 says that the Father has given judgment to the Son. 2 Timothy 4:1 says that Jesus will judge the living and the dead. All of us, small and great, will stand before God in that judgment, just as Pilate did.

And what of Jesus? His case was appealed to a higher court. It was appealed to the highest court of all. God exonerated Jesus by the resurrection. It proved He was who He claimed to be. God exonerated Jesus in the ascension. It proved that He was accepted by God. God exonerated Jesus when He had Him sit at His own right hand.

Jesus' case was also taken to another court: the court of human opinion. What's the verdict there? Daniel Webster said, "He is a superhuman Savior." Renan, the French historian, said, "He is the cornerstone of history." Wells wrote, "He was too large for our small hearts." So say they all! So say I! What say you? For you, ladies and gentlemen, are the jury. You must bring in a verdict on Jesus. What say you?

The Text That Comforted Jesus

Do you have a favorite text? Most people do. In Eastern Europe each person selects a text before his baptism and that is his or her special text. Jesus had some favorite texts. He quoted them more than once. They must have been His favorites. There is a text that comforted Jesus on the cross. While it is only quoted once in the gospels, it must have been a favorite because of the circumstances in which He quoted it.

It is possible to picture the scene at Golgotha. For three hours Jesus has suffered under the blistering sun. Then God seemed to say, "Enough!" He drew a curtain of darkness over the whole earth. Out of the darkness there came that haunting, piercing, puzzling cry: "My God! My God! Why has thou forsaken me?"

It *is* puzzling, isn't it? Can it be that God had really forsaken Jesus? On the other hand, can it be that Jesus was mistaken?

Some say the answer lies in 2 Corinthians 5:21. Other texts tell us that He bore our sins, but that verse says He *became* sin. If that is to be taken literally, then how could a holy God look upon sin? It is argued that when Jesus became sin for us God had to turn away for a moment, and in that moment the cry comes. If such a view is correct it shows us the enormity of sin. It shows us that sin is no trifling matter. If sin could separate the

Son from the Father, it is no triviality! If that view is true it shows us the enormity of the price paid for our redemption. If Jesus had to be separated from God, even for an instant, the price was enormous. If that view is true it shows us the enormity of God's love, and of Christ's love, too.

While that view may be true, there is another interpretation that is much simpler and much nearer at hand. The words of Jesus are identical to the first verse of Psalm 22. Perhaps Jesus was quoting Scripture on the cross. Perhaps He quoted the whole psalm and those nearby heard only the first part of it.

Jesus often quoted Scripture. He quoted Scripture when He was tempted on the mountain after His baptism. Again and again He met Satan's offers with Scripture. Do you ever quote Scripture when you are tempted? Do you *know* enough Scripture to quote it when you are tempted? David did. He said, "Thy word have I hid in mine heart, that I might not sin against thee."

In His debates with His enemies Jesus often quoted Scripture. "Have you not read?" He asked. "Have you not read?"

A man said that once he passed through a dark and awful night. Nameless fears gripped him. He was filled with anxiety and dread. He said that he was sustained through that dark night of the soul by quoting to himself all the Scripture he could remember. Much of it he had learned in his youth. He quoted it to himself over and over again and he was sustained by it.

So it fits all we know about Jesus to suppose that He was quoting Scripture on the cross. And that Scripture, Psalm 22, certainly fits what was happening on the cross. Look at verse 7: "All who see me mock at me, they make mouths at me, they wag their heads; he committed his cause to the Lord; let him deliver him, let him rescue him, for he delights in him!" *(RSV)*. You can hear the very echo of that in the taunts they hurled at Jesus on the cross. Look at verse 14: "I am poured out like water, and all my bones are out of joint. My heart has turned to wax; it has melted away within me" *(NIV)*. And verse 16: "They have pierced my hands and feet." It sounds like an account by an eyewitness, but it is a prophecy written hundreds of years before. And verse 18: "They divide my garments among them and cast lots for my clothing." Every ring of the hammer, every shout of the scribes, every deed of the soldiers was a fulfillment of prophecy . . . and a fulfillment of Psalm 22.

Psalm 22 begins with that cry from the cross, "My God! My God! Why hast thou forsaken me?" I think the emphasis was on the word "Thou." He knew why men had forsaken Him. He could see His disciples watching from afar, just as they could see Him. He knew their frame. He remembered that they were dust. He knew how fear had chilled their hearts. He knew why men had forsaken Him. I think the cry was, "Why hast *Thou* forsaken me?" And if this Psalm fits perfectly Jesus' crucifixion, this cry fits perfectly our experience. Surely everyone cries out at some point in life, "Why?" The hard questions of life are always the *Why* questions. We can answer the questions that begin with Who, What, Where, and When. It's the Why questions that puzzle us. Dostoevsky said that we can manage the how of life if only we have a why.

In a village cemetery in Austria there is a one word epitaph. The stone marks the burial place of a child. The stone gives his name, the date of birth, the date of death, and then this epitaph — one word — "*Warum*" — Why? Out of the depths of our own Gethsemanes and Golgothas we cry, "Why?"

We ought not to feel guilty in asking that question. We have every right to ask it. If Jesus asked it on the cross it cannot be wrong for us to ask it, too. But in asking, we must not assume that we will always get an answer. We may get an answer, we may not. And if we do not get an answer, we must not assume that there is no answer. It may only mean that we are not yet ready to receive the answer; that it lies hidden in the wise heart of God.

Was Jesus forsaken on the cross? No. Did He feel forsaken on the cross? Yes. Are we ever forsaken? Never! Do we sometimes feel forsaken? Yes. But notice that even when Jesus felt forsaken He did not stop believing in God. His response was a prayer. Neither David who wrote the Psalm, nor Jesus who quoted it, stopped believing in God. We sometimes do that in our disappointment. When life goes wrong we sometimes conclude that there just isn't any God. But Jesus did not stop believing in God, nor did He stop believing in prayer. We sometimes say, "Why pray? It doesn't do any good. It's no use to pray." But even on the cross Jesus still believed in prayer. And even on the cross Jesus still believed that God was His Father. This cry lies between the two prayers from the cross. Both of them begin with the word, "Father." "Father, forgive them, for they know not what they do" and "Father, into Thy hands I commit my spirit." Jesus never stopped believing in God, in prayer, or that God was a Father. And we must never stop believing in God, in prayer, or in the fatherhood of God.

Imagine a piece of paper saying to a writer, "Why are you making all those marks on me. I was pretty and clean, and now I'm all marked up. And besides that, your pen scratches and it hurts." But the writer will say to the paper, "You are only a piece of paper. When I get through with you, you will be a masterpiece. You are worth very little now, but when I am through with you you will be worth ten thousand times more."

Imagine the clay speaking to the sculptor. "Stop pinching me! You're squeezing me too tightly. And those tools are sharp. It hurts!" But the sculptor will answer, "You are just a lump of clay. When I am through with you you will be a lovely piece of art and people will admire you for generations."

Imagine the gold saying to the jeweler, "Don't put me in the fire! I don't like the fire! Whatever you do, don't put me in the fire!" And the jeweler will say, "Only if you go through the fire can you become the beautiful thing I want to make out of you."

If ever you have to go through the fire, if ever you feel squeezed in by life, if you get marked and scratched, remember that it may be God is trying to make something out of you.

Suppose Jesus had not gone to the cross. Suppose that a magic carpet had whisked Him from the courtroom. Suppose He had never felt the whip, the thorns, the nails, the spear? Would there be any Christian religion at all? We'd have to take half the songs out of our hymnbook. We'd have to take half the texts out of our Bible. There would be no Communion table. There would be no baptism. In truth, there would be no church, for we are drawn by the magnetism of the cross. It drew us to God and it drew us together.

So, when you have to take up your cross, just remember that you are only a lump of clay now, but God is going to make something out of you.

When Columbus first landed in the New World, he waded ashore carrying a cross. He stuck it in the sand and claimed that land in the name of the king of Spain *and* in the name of the Christ who was symbolized by that cross. Almost every place he discovered he named for a saint or a holy day.

So Christ comes into your life with a cross. He says, "I claim this life by virtue of my cross." Are you going to acknowledge His claim?

The Gospel According to Psalm 118

We are all familiar with the three R's, but try explaining that to someone for whom English is a second language! Writing and Arithmetic don't begin with R. The person who coined the phrase should have taken a fourth course: Spelling. Still, it's proverbial now to speak of the three R's, and there are three in this text (Psalm 118:22, 23). There is the rejection of Christ, the raising up of Christ, and the reign of Christ.

In the parable of the vineyard, Jesus spoke of a man who sent servants to check on his vineyard. They beat his servants and drove them off. So, he sent his son. They killed him. Just after telling that parable Jesus quoted Psalm 118. "The rejected stone is become the head of the corner."

When Peter and John were threatened and told never again to preach in the name of Jesus. They said they had to obey God rather than men. Then *they* quoted this text from Psalm 118. When Peter wrote that lovely book, which nearly brings to a close our New Testament, he commented on this text.

Let's look first at the rejection of Christ. They rejected Christ as a teacher. They would not accept His truth. They would not accept His view of life. Instead, they tried to argue with Him! There was the all-wise Lord of the universe, revealing profound truth to finite human beings, and they argued with Him! They rejected Him as a teacher.

They rejected Him as their Lord, like the Hebrews long ago who said to Moses, "Who made thee a lord and divider over us?" "By what authority doest thou these things?" they challenged Jesus. They would not accept His lordship over their lives. The story of their rejection is written so poignantly in the first chapter of John. "He came unto his own, and his own received him not." We might have accepted it if He had been rejected by strangers, but "he came unto his own and his own received him not." That goes to the heart! He came unto His own world, the world of His creation: the world formed by His fingers, the world sustained by His power. His world received Him not.

He came unto people made in His own image, into whose nostrils He had breathed the very breath of life. They would not have Him.

He came unto His own nation; a nation whose spiritual expectancy had been honed to a fine edge. They looked for a deliverer and did not know Him when He came.

He came to His own hometown, to the streets where He'd played as a boy, to the very synagogue where as a youth He had studied the Scriptures, to the very people who had known Him all His life. When He declared himself to them, they dragged Him from the synagogue and tried to kill Him. He came unto His own village and they received Him not.

The ultimate rejection of Jesus did not occur when they argued with His teaching, when they refused to accept His lordship, or when they dragged Him from the hometown synagogue at Nazareth. The ultimate rejection was at Calvary, where they nailed Him on a cross and lifted Him up as a spectacle. Have you ever pondered the reason why? We cry out with Pilate, "Why? What evil hath He done?" What was it in the hearts of men that drove them to destroy Jesus? He had committed no crime. He had done no sin. He had harmed no one. His whole life had been devoted to doing good. Why? Why? What was in the hearts of men that caused them to nail Jesus to a cross? The question has already been answered. His very perfection spelled His doom. Our world is so evil it cannot abide perfection. If ever there should come again a perfect man, the world would destroy Him, too. It was His very sinlessness they could not abide.

If they could have recalled a sin He'd done or a mistake He'd made, they might have let him live. Finding none, this sinful broken world in which we live drove perfection to the cross. We had better be thankful that none of us will achieve sinless perfection. If you ever got to that place they'd do the same thing to you! The nearer you come to it, the more you're going to experience the world's rejection. The purer you are, the deeper will be the world's rejection of you.

The cross was the ultimate rejection of Christ. We marvel at it until we come across that poem by Studdert-Kennedy:

When Jesus came to Golgotha
They hanged him on a tree.
They drove great nails through hands and feet
And made a Calvary.

A crown of thorns was on his head.
Red were his wounds and deep.
For those were crude and cruel days
And human flesh was cheap.

When Jesus came to Birmingham
They simply passed him by.
They never hurt a hair on him.
They only let him die.

And then in the last verse of that moving poem the author pictures Jesus in the cold rain, crouching against a wall facing our rejection and longing instead for Calvary. Studdert-Kennedy thought Jesus would prefer the suffering of Calvary to the cold indifference of our rejection. Perhaps such a view is too extreme, but the author was certain that Jesus would prefer to go to the cross again rather than face *our* rejection of Him—*our* rejection of His teaching, *our* rejection of His lordship, *our* rejection of His place in our lives. To one man it seemed that Calvary was not so painful as that.

We make fun of the pagan bowing before His image and bringing food and flowers to a dumb idol, and yet does not that mark more reverence for his handmade god than we hold for the creator of Heaven and earth? Doesn't that pagan revere more highly the nonsensical laws of his idolatrous religion than we revere the wisely given laws of ours?

Rejection! Not a pleasant story, but a story that must be told. But the stone the builders rejected has been raised up and made the head of the corner! The cornerstone was no formality then. It was the very instrument by which the building was squared and leveled. It was the one true stone by which all others were judged. That was the cornerstone!

This text came to me often in my youth. Not only did Jesus quote this text, my mother quoted it to me over and over. Her application was somewhat different than that which we see in Scripture. If there was an individual who had been passed over and then finally recognized, my mother's comment would be, "The rejected stone is become the head of the corner." If some object thought useless suddenly turned out to have value after all, some broken tool you almost threw away, then she'd quote this verse. She meant no disrespect for Scripture. Yet here is a proverb that belongs in a much higher realm than any human experience. There is no human event that is halfway worthy of this splendid verse. It applies to Jesus and to Jesus alone! When men had done all that they could do to Him, God reached into that damp tomb and brought Him forth. He broke the bonds that bind us all. Death was no match for Him. His resurrection is the lifting up of the rejected stone. God did not reject that which men disallowed.

On a day in January in 1977, thousands upon thousands of pilgrims streamed across the face of India. They were all bound for a single city—the city where the Jumna and the Ganges rivers come together. To them that is the holiest spot on earth. And that day was the holiest day in history. On that day, they said, all the heavenly bodies were in exactly the same configuration as they were at the dawn of Creation. Thousands bathed in the river to wash away their sins. But they were mistaken. The holiest day in history was not a day in January, 1977. It was the day of the resurrection when Jesus Christ came forth from the grave. That was history's holiest day.

196

Celsus was the first great skeptic. He once asked, "What has Jesus given to the world that no one else has given?" Someone answered, "Himself!" Yes, that's Jesus' magnificent, stunning gift to the world. He gave himself! Not only did He give himself in submission upon the cross, but in power at the resurrection.

But the raising up of Christ goes beyond the resurrection. That's part of it; an essential part of it. But the raising of Jesus did not end with the resurrection. That's where it began. Having raised Him from the dead, God raised Him from the earth, raised Him to Heaven itself, and Jesus sat down on the right hand of God. "Wherefore God also hath highly exalted him, and given him a name which is above every name: that at the name of Jesus every knee should bow . . ." (Philippians 2:9, 10)

There is no way to imagine it. The resurrection we can picture. We can see two men walking down a dusty road with a "stranger." We can see the disciples huddled in fear behind locked doors and Jesus appearing in the midst. We can picture them fishing on the Sea of Galilee and then joining Jesus for breakfast by a bonfire on the shore. All of that we can imagine. But when the conquering hero returned to glory, when the Son came back to the bosom of the Father, when the eternal Word was once more in the eternal city, what then? Some say Psalm 24 pictures that occasion.

Lift up your heads, O ye gates;
and be ye lifted up, ye everlasting doors,
and the King of glory shall come in.
Who is this King of glory?
The Lord strong and mighty,
the Lord mighty in battle . . .
he is the King of glory."
(Psalm 24:7-10)

That, say some, is the fanfare. That, say some, is the processional march when Jesus came home.

It was three precious scenes rolled into one. It was homecoming. We've all experienced that; the table ready, all the favorite dishes prepared, all the good times of old remembered. Friends come, and it's a time of joy and festivity. Homecoming!

197

The second picture is reunion. I've been to some family reunions. It's such a pleasure. It's a simple, yet profound joy. Some come from afar. Some have been away for years. It is a time of renewal and rejoicing.

The third picture is that of coronation. Perhaps you watched on television the coronation of Queen Elizabeth II. Then you watched the 25th anniversary of it, too. She rode again in the golden coach in which she'd ridden a quarter of a century before. It was a great, happy, solemn day.

Take the best of all three pictures, put them together, multiply them ten thousand times, and you have some notion of the exaltation of Jesus. From that place He now rules the world. Sixty-three people have sat on the throne of England if you don't count Oliver Cromwell. Fifty-eight kings and five queens have ruled England. But only one King has ever sat where Jesus sits. None sat there before Him. None will sit there after Him. Forever He reigns there, not as king of a nation, nor an empire. nor a planet, but as the King of all that is! One can count twenty who sat on the throne in Jerusalem. In the new Jerusalem only one King has ever ruled, . . . or ever shall! Don't forget that third R. *Rejected* by men, *raised* by God, Christ is *ruling* now! He will continue to rule forever.

When Queen Elizabeth was crowned they brought to her a sceptre. On the top of it was the star of Africa, the largest diamond in the world. Before that they brought to her a staff. On the top of that staff was a dove, a symbol of their prayer that the Holy Spirit would be her guide. But before that they brought to her a ring, like a wedding ring. It symbolized the union between the queen and her people. But before that they brought to her an orb. It was a globe of the world made of solid pure gold. And over it there was a cross. It said, even to the queen, "It is Christ who rules the world. It is not you, nor any other mortal. It is Christ who rules the world!" When Peter and John used this verse to defend their right to preach, they went on to say, "Neither is there salvation in any other: for there is none other name under Heaven given among men, whereby we must be saved, (Acts 4:12). Christ stands in an absolutely exclusive position. No one can take His place!

There is no salvation in any other name. There is no salvation in Buddha. There is no salvation in Mohammed. There is no salvation in Zoroaster. There is no salvation in Confucius. There is no salvation in Sun Myung Moon. There is no salvation in any name but His!

If you do not acknowledge His exclusive right, you do not acknowledge Him at all. He will not take His place in some pantheon of gods. He stands alone.

There really is a fourth R to our religion. I want only to suggest it. It is *Returning*. The Christ, rejected by men, raised by God, ruling over the world, is returning. Two little girls were playing church. One was playing preacher. She was preaching on the return of Christ. She said, "Jesus is coming back again. Maybe today. Maybe tomorrow. Maybe never." We smile at it because we know that the one absolute certainty is that Jesus is coming back again. The one haunting question is, "Are you ready for Him?"

The Inescapable Christ

There were two failures on Easter Day. The first is the failure of Easter morning related in Matthew 27:66 and 28:1-6. The second is the failure of Easter night related in John 20:19. The first was the failure to seal Christ in. The second was the failure to shut Christ out. The sealed tomb could not keep Jesus in on Easter morning. The shut door could not keep Jesus out on Easter night. But the subject is not the failure of man to seal Him in or shut Him out. The subject is the inescapable Christ—the Christ from whom you can never entirely get away.

One of the most interesting characters in American life is Harry Houdini, the great magician. He used to have himself handcuffed, chained, padlocked, put into a chest, the chest nailed shut and then that thrown into the sea. He would emerge unscathed. It's no problem to understand that if you've read the life of Harry Houdini. First, he became an expert on locks. He knew more about them than the people who made them. Then he learned how to expand his body so that when they bound him with chains his body was puffed up larger. Inside the chest he would contract the muscles and make himself smaller and slide right out. He learned how to pull out the nails in the lid of the chest from the inside. When that chest hit the water, he was already free inside of it and had only to burst forth and swim to the surface.

It's no problem to understand that, though it took Houdini years to learn how to do it.

With Christ in the tomb you have a wholly different proposition. They put a seal on the tomb. It was only a piece of wax, but behind it lay all the power of Rome, the most powerful nation then on earth. Its armies had never known defeat. It stretched to the outer edges of civilization. That most powerful of nations could not keep Christ in His tomb.

Some years after Christ one of His followers was about to be executed. Taunting him, a Roman soldier said, "Where is your carpenter now?" The Christian replied, "He is out in the world, building a coffin for the Empire." That's exactly what that carpenter did. Not only did Christ break the seal of Rome, He broke the power of Rome. After a few years, the very city that had been the seat of Roman political power became the capital of the church.

In our own day, Communism is trying to do what Rome failed to do, but Communism is failing, too. Churches in the western world are crowded on Easter. In the Communist world they are crowded every Sunday. Every service is packed with people standing in the aisles and around the walls. They tried to seal Christ in, but they have failed and the church is strong still.

Nature could not keep him in. That stone was a solid wheel of stone that lay in a trench. One could roll it down the trench and before the opening, thus closing the door of the tomb. But in order to roll it you had to be on the outside, where you could get your shoulder against it.

Some say that Jesus only went into a coma on the cross. They say that He revived in the coolness of the tomb, pushed the stone away and came out. But remember Christ had been severely beaten. He had been pierced in head and hands and feet and side. The loss of blood was enormous. He hung on the cross for six hours. Is it possible to believe that this beaten, weak, semi-comatose man was strong enough to roll back the stone, *from the inside*? Three strong, healthy women didn't think they could do it *from the outside!* How was it possible for Him to do it from the inside? It was impossible, except there be a miracle! We talk about the empty tomb, but the tomb was not empty. There was something in it. It was the graveclothes. You know how they prepared a body for burial in those days. They put the body in a winding sheet. It was like a very long and very large bandage. They wound it round and round like the mummies in ancient Egypt. Is it possible to believe that this semi-comatose man got out of that winding sheet *from the inside?* It was impossible, except there be a miracle.

Death itself could not keep Jesus in. He truly died, and He was truly raised from the dead. Death seems to us so strong, so final, so irrevocable. Death seems to us to end all things, but death could not keep Him prisoner.

But there is a strange thing here. In the Bible it was the enemies of Jesus who tried to seal Him in. In life, it is His friends who try to seal Him in. We try to seal Him in our human organizations. We try to monopolize Him. We think that anyone who wants Him must go through us. We confine Him to our understanding of the Christian gospel. But is there one of us who understands it perfectly? We cannot confine Him. We cannot lock Him away in a church building, supposing that we can see Him when we need Him but that He will not interfere when we don't want Him. We like to think we know where to find Him, but we don't want to worry about confronting Him at some embarrassing moment in life. But all our efforts to contain Christ fail. He keeps confronting us, even in places where we didn't expect to find Him. He is alive and loose in the world and neither His friends nor His enemies can seal him in.

As He could not be sealed in, so He could not be shut out. His disciples had no intention of shutting Him out. There were others they wanted to shut out. They didn't realize that in shutting out others, they were shutting Him out, too.

Is there someone you are shutting out of your life? Perhaps it's someone in your family, or a friend, or an enemy. The disciples only wanted to shut out their enemies, but in shutting out their enemies they also were shutting out Christ. But Christ came through those closed doors. When He did, He opened up the way for others to come in, too. In the same way He'll burst into your life. He's not going to let you shut Him out. When He comes in He's going to open up a way for all the people you tried to shut out. Perhaps they were people with needs and you didn't want to be bothered about them. Perhaps they were people who were hurting and you didn't want to take the time to help. All the people you try to shut out are going to come in. Just as Christ breaks open the door to life, so He breaks open the door to the church.

We try to shut Him out by our selfishness. Suddenly, we are confronted with a truly unselfish person who does a truly unselfish deed—for us. Then all our barriers come down. Sometimes through our bitterness we try to shut Him out. A very cultured and well-educated lady once asked, "Why does God let innocent people suffer?" I'm not sure I answered it very well at the time. But I do know now what I should have said. For the answer is another question. "Why does God let us enjoy undeserved love and goodness? Why are there those who do for others great and heroic and unselfish deeds?" She can no more answer my question than I can answer hers.

The second part of the response is this: God suffers. That may not help us to understand it, but it does help us to accept it. There must be a good reason for it, if God himself suffers. In our bitterness we try to shut Christ out, but in the sweetness of His grace He melts our defenses.

Compromise can shut Him out. We make so many of them. Then we are confronted with someone who cannot compromise right and wrong, and who will not. In that firmness we are confronted with Christ again. In our disbelief we try to shut Him out and He just piles up the evidence.

Perhaps you have been to Washington, D.C. Perhaps you've climbed up all those stairs to the top of the Washington monument. As you climbed up the dark interior of that stairway, now and then you came across a little window—not very big, but big enough to let some shafts of light into the dark interior and big enough to let you look out and enjoy the view. That's the way it works. We live our lives shrouded by darkness, and yet Christ keeps shining little shafts of light in upon us. They dispel for a time the darkness and open up for us new views of life and the world and Heaven itself!

Science tells us that in the long process of evolution from non-living things there came living things . . . and from non-reasoning things there came reasoning things. Then we are asked to deny that from us living things there may come to be eternal things. How can men accept one and reject the other?

If it is in any sense reasonable to think that the living came from the non-living, how much more reasonable to think that from the living there should come the eternal.

Are we to suppose that all the promises of the Bible are only so many worthless checks and that we must come back from the bank empty-handed? Are those promises like the gold stock or the oil stock that people bought years ago, and all they had to show for their investment was a piece of paper?

There is a wing on the bird. Is it conceivable that there should be no air for it to beat against? There is a fin on the fish. Is it conceivable that there should be no water for it to brush against? Man has this deep longing for eternity. Is it conceivable that there is no eternity?

Look at yourself. You know that you were not made for this world. You know you were made for something better and more lasting. The evidence is everywhere. And neither our selfishness, nor our bitterness, nor our compromises, nor our disbelief can ever finally shut Christ out. He keeps bursting into your life, crying, "Believe! Believe!"

Do you remember the story of the ugly duckling? He didn't walk like a duck, he didn't quack like a duck, and he didn't look like a duck, but he lived among the ducks in the barnyard. Then one fine day, he heard a call from above. He had never heard it before, but in him was an instinct that answered that call. In the sky he saw a speck. The speck became a long trail. The call became louder and more insistent. The ugly duckling began to flap his wings. He found that he could fly. Up above the barnyard, higher and higher he flew, to answer that call and to join that company. He disappeared from the barnyard. The ducks never saw him again. They said that he died, but we know better. "They that wait upon the Lord shall renew their strength. They shall mount up with wings as eagles."

Sunset, Sunrise

"Sunrise, sunset. Sunrise, sunset." That song was made familiar to us in the play, "Fiddler on the Roof." Today's text is just the opposite of that. It is not sunrise that fades into sunset but it is sunset that is miraculously turned into dawn. You see that in Luke 24:13-35.

You can tell a lot about a person by the way he walks. You can tell the kind of mood he is in. If you could have seen these followers of Jesus on their outward journey from Jerusalem and seen them again on their return trip, you would have known that something had happened. There was a spring in their step.

It was many years after our children were grown that I learned they had a special name for the way I used to walk during our vacations. Vacation time was the only time I wore sneakers. That, plus the exhilaration of not having to go to work, gave a certain spring to my step. I learned years later my children called it "the vacation bounce." They knew good times were ahead when they saw Dad walking with the vacation bounce.

There was a spring in the step of these disciples of the Lord after they had seen Him. They found a new way of walking. Going out to Emmaus, they were dragging their feet. Going back, they walked with vigor and joy.

Then there was also something new about the way they walked because they traveled slowly on the way out from Jerusalem, discussing their disappointment. When they had seen the risen Lord, they came back with haste. They hurried with the good news.

They learned a new way of walking. Paul said, "If you are risen with Christ seek those things which are above." The resurrected Christ leads us to walk in new paths, to walk in His footsteps. All of it is symbolized in a simple fact. Before they met the risen Lord, they were facing west toward the sunset. After having met the risen Lord, they were facing east toward the sunrise. All Moslem mosques, wherever they are in the world, face Mecca. It used to be that every synagogue faced Jerusalem. We don't worry about the orientation of the building, but the orientation of life is terribly significant. We are facing east. We are facing the sunrise. We are facing the dawning of a new day.

On their outward journey from Jerusalem, they were talking in the past tense—"We had hoped," they said, "that He would redeem Israel." Until they knew that the resurrection was real, all their religion was in the past tense. There are a great many people whose religion is altogether in the past. They will tell you of all the wonderful things that have happened in the days gone by. They have no enthusiasm for the present and no hope for the future. They are just like these disciples who had not yet met the risen Lord. All of their religion was in the past tense, but when they knew Jesus had come back from the dead, they changed their way of talking. It came out of the past tense into the present tense and into the future. That's where we must live and work—in the present tense with an eye on the future. Before they met the risen Christ, they talked about their doubts. Doubt is a common thing. Even among those who believe there are transient doubts, but these disciples that were speaking of their doubts on their outward journey were speaking of their faith on the return journey.

Whatever doubts may come to take up temporary residence in our hearts, the theme of our conversation must not be our doubts but our faith. One thing was not changed in their conversation. The subject was the same on both journeys: Jesus Christ. When you lift up Christ, nobody can criticize Him. People criticize the church, but when you lift up Christ, they have nothing to say. Everyone must agree with Pontius Pilate, "I find no fault in him." Let Christ be the subject of our conversation, our teaching, our preaching, our singing, and everything we do.

These disciples learned a new way of walking. They learned a new way of talking. They learned a new way of thinking. When they met Christ on the road, they did not recognize Him. Many explanations have been offered for this. Some have said that since they were facing the setting sun, the sun blinded their eyes. Some say they were still weeping over a lost cause and through their tears they did not recognize Christ. Some people say that the resurrected Christ looked different than the Christ they had known during His ministry. In fact, it was a miracle that Jesus performed. He performed it for a very significant purpose. He did not want their faith to rest on the foundation of experience. He wanted it to rest on the foundation of Scripture. When He got through explaining the Scriptures to them, they believed in the resurrection. It was before their eyes were opened! Their faith rested on the Word of God. That's the foundation for our faith, too. It is not our experience but the Word of God.

On a snowy night in Budapest, Hungary, after I had taught for about two hours, a young lady came up from the back. Through the interpreter she introduced herself to me. I will change her name. She said. "My name is Juanita and I am a Communist." Now, nobody ever before looked me in the eye and said, "I am a Communist." It was a rather startling experience. She was from Cuba. She had come to study in Hungary, but lately some events that happened in her life caused her to wonder if there might be a God. To be a Communist, you must be an atheist. It is absolutely required everywhere except in the United States and Great Britain. She said, "My mother and father are Communists," but lately some events had caused her to wonder if there might be a God.

I was standing there wondering what to say. I had one chance and only one. It was late. It was getting dark. It was snowing. I had miles to travel. I knew that I had only a few minutes and I did not know what to say. So, I fell back upon something that I had been teaching that very day from the book of Romans.

"Faith comes by hearing, and hearing by the word of God." I said, "You must read the Bible. Don't worry about the parts you don't understand, just read it, and as you read it, ask yourself, 'Is it possible that it is true?'" She thought that she didn't want to do that. She just wanted to wait and see what other experiences might lead her to think that there was a God. I said, "No, you must read the Bible. Don't worry about the parts you don't understand. Just read it, and you will come to faith." I don't know if I gave her the right answer or not. When I left she was still there chatting with the believers. It's cold in the Communist world in more ways than one and she was enjoying the warmth of Christian fellowship, but I believe I gave her the right answer. No one had richer spiritual experiences than the apostle Paul, yet he said, "Faith comes by hearing and hearing by the word of God." No one had richer spiritual experiences than Peter, yet when he spoke of them he went on to say that we should rely upon the word of God (1 Peter 1:17-19).

Jesus wanted their *faith* to rest on Scripture, not on experience. He wants our *doctrine* to rest on Scripture and not on experience. Often I talk with people whose experiences are not identical to what you read in the New Testament. I do not propose to question their experience. I do question that we should build our doctrine on their experience or on my experience or your experience or anybody else's experience. Let us build our doctrine on the Word of God.

Jesus wanted their enthusiasm to rest on the Word of God. "Did not our heart burn within us, while he talked with us by the way, and while he opened to us the Scriptures?" This is the source of our enthusiasm. We cannot just drum up enthusiasm. Enthusiasm that is worked up cheerleader style will not endure. A pep rally is not enough for those who would march in the Lord's army. We have to have an enthusiasm that is built on the Word of God.

That is why He would not let them recognize Him until first He could explain the Scriptures. When He had explained the Scripture, their eyes were opened and they knew that it was He. So, they discovered a new way of thinking and a new way of living. For now they lived as men who had a destiny. They knew when they left Jerusalem their destination. It was the village of

Emmaus. They did not know yet their destiny. They thought, they wondered, they hoped but after having learned the Scriptures from the Lord, they knew that they had a destiny.

That's a wonderful question somebody asked. "Where are you going to be when you get where you're going?" Oh, how I would like to ask that question of the people who race up and down our highways – "Where are you going to be when you get where you are going?" Well, some of us are going home. Thank God, some of us are going home.

It's fascinating to consider how many of the great dramatic events of the Bible occurred on the highway. We can almost borrow a little phrase from Charles Kuralt and talk about, "On the Road with Jesus Christ." On the road someday you perhaps will chance to meet Him, too. Will your eyes be open that you will know Him? Will you listen as He opens to you the Scripture? Will you have an enthusiasm, an understanding, and a faith that is built on the Word of God?

We had in our church in Largo, Florida, a delightful Christian man who had spent years as a carny man. Chick Wagner started out as a boxer in the little carnivals that went around from county fair to county fair in Ohio and Indiana. He had a cauliflower ear to prove it. Then he rode a motorcycle in the Drome of Death. After that he had a little concession where you could try your luck at shooting a basketball into a goal. In Indiana and Ohio all those young farm boys think that they can do that very well. For thirty years he traveled on the road every summer. The rest of the year he was in Florida and he was in our church. When he was on the road he was in church, too, and would often send me a bulletin from somewhere – never a word, never a letter, never a return address on the envelope. I would just get a church bulletin from somewhere in Ohio or somewhere in Indiana, and I knew that Chick Wagner had been there. Every spring when he left, he would ask my wife to sing, "When I've Gone the Last Mile of the Way." He did that every year. One year, on the highway, on his way to a county fair, he had a little problem with the trailer. He pulled off to the side of the road, had a heart attack and died – on the road. He had gone the last mile of the way. He had not traveled it alone!

Come and Dine

On the last page of his Gospel, John paints for us one of the most enchanting pictures in the New Testament. It is the morning after the resurrection. The disciples of Jesus, Peter and his friends, had gone back to their old profession of fishing. Early in the morning Jesus met them by the sea.

> He called out to them, "Friends, haven't you any fish?"
> "No," they answered.
> He said, "Throw your net on the right side of the boat and you will find some." When they did, they were unable to haul the net in because of the large number of fish.
> Then the disciple whom Jesus loved said to Peter, "It is the Lord!" As soon as Simon Peter heard him say, "It is the Lord," he wrapped his outer garment around him (for he had taken it off) and jumped into the water.
>
> (John 21:5-7, *NIV*)

Have you ever tried to swim with your clothes on? The apostle Peter, out of his respect for the Lord, would not stand before him as he did before his fellows. He put on his garments to meet Jesus.

But the other disciples came in the little boat. For they were not far from the land, but about 100 yards away, dragging the net full of fish. So, when they got out upon the land they saw a charcoal fire already laid and fish placed on it and bread.

Jesus said to them, "Bring some of the fish that you have just caught."

Simon Peter climbed aboard and dragged the net ashore. It was full of large fish, 153, but even with so many the net was not torn. Jesus said to them, "Come and have breakfast."

(John 21:10-12a, *NIV*)

We are impressed that the resurrected Lord would put aside for awhile the pressing business of the kingdom to fix breakfast for His disciples by the sea. Some of us are in such a hurry we don't even eat breakfast at all. The resurrected Christ not only had time to eat breakfast, but He had time to fix breakfast for the disciples.

A long time ago somebody said to me, "I never read where God got in a hurry." Dorothy Sayers wrote, "We cannot imagine Jesus hurrying. We cannot imagine Paul not hurrying." We are impressed here with the unhurried Christ.

In only a few days He would say to the disciples, "Wait." That must have been the most difficult command He ever gave them: "Wait." They were caught up in the enthusiasm of the resurrection. They were anxious to go and preach the gospel to every creature. Their hearts burned with the message. He said to them, "Wait."

Between the ascension of our Lord and the day of Pentecost when the church began, there were ten days. During those ten days, the disciples had to wait and to pray. The Lord gave them a ten-day vacation.

Once a minister was criticized by a member of his church for taking a vacation. The member said, "How can you take a vacation from the Lord's work? Don't you know the Devil never takes a vacation?"

The minister said, "Yes. That's what makes him so mean."

The disciples got a ten day vacation. So, we see the unhurried Christ. We see the humble Christ who builds the fire and cleans the fish and cooks the breakfast. Some ladies are married to fishermen. Let me ask you, who cleans the fish? Everybody likes to catch fish. Everybody likes to eat fish. Nobody likes to clean fish. Jesus did it!

We want to see not only Christ here, but those others gathered about the fire. We want to see ourselves here. Let us sit down on a stone or squat by the fire and see if we can get the feel of this situation. Do you think it was a solemn occasion? Do you think it was a joyous occasion? Do you think they slapped each other on the back and laughed? Or do you think they sat in reverent awe of the miracle that they had seen?

What do you think they talked about that morning by the sea? Do you think they talked about theology? Do you think that they discussed some great doctrine and asked Jesus to explain the finer points of it? Do you think they talked about evangelism and made their plans for telling others about the resurrection? Do you think they decided who would go east and who would go west and how the job would be done?

Perhaps they made small talk; the kind of small talk people make when there are weighty subjects on their minds, but they are not yet ready to discuss them. Maybe they made small talk. Maybe they talked about the weather and the fish. Maybe they wondered if they had ever caught bigger or tasted better.

Perhaps they said nothing at all. Perhaps the meal was eaten in silence; an embarrassed silence or a reverent silence. Perhaps the only sounds were the crackling of the fire and the slapping of the waves on the rocks. We don't know, of course. Your guess is as good as mine. But it's good for us to speculate about it.

We have only one little slice of conversation out of that event, and that was perhaps a private conversation between Jesus and Peter.

Jesus said, "Do you love me?"

Peter said, "You know I love you."

Jesus said, "Feed my sheep."

Beyond that we do not know what conversation took place, if any.

But we do know this. This was one of those rare occasions when Jesus was the host. Often Jesus was the guest. He was the guest of Mary, Martha, and Lazarus at Bethany. He was the guest of Simon. He was the guest of Zacchaeus. He was guest of many another. Often He was the guest. Seldom was He the host.

I can think of one event before this one in which Jesus was the host. It was that night in the upper room when they celebrated the Passover and He gave the Lord's supper to His disciples and to us. I can think of one subsequent to this when Jesus was the host. It happened here *this morning* just a few moments ago. For when it was time for *us* to eat *this* bread and drink of *this* cup, Jesus said, "Come and dine." He was here. I know that He was here because He said that He would be here. Jesus always keeps His promises. He was not counted when the ushers counted the attendance. He didn't fill out an attendance card and hand it in. No one saw Him. No door turned upon its hinges when He entered. He passed through closed doors here as He did in an upper room in Jerusalem long ago. But He was here. And He gave us the invitation just as He gave it by the sea long ago— "Come and dine."

Suppose you had been alive in the time of our Lord. Suppose that this morning He had awakened you from sleep and said, "Wake up! Wake up! I'm going down to the sea to cook breakfast for the disciples and I want you to go with me." Is there a person here who would have refused the invitation? Is there a person here who would have said, "Oh, I'm so tired I think I would rather sleep in." Why, we would have given anything or every- thing to have had *that* invitation long ago. "Come and dine."

Does *this* invitation mean less than that one? Have you ever wanted to go someplace and couldn't because you didn't get an invitation? Every one of us has had that experience at some point of life. Maybe you were a child. The kids in the neighbor- hood had a birthday party. You wanted to go, but you weren't invited. You remember the pain of it to this very day. Perhaps it was something far more recent than that and more significant than that. You wanted to go but you couldn't because you didn't get an invitation, and you still bear the scars of it.

On the other hand, have you had the experience of extending an invitation to someone and having it spurned? Can you not remember the pain of that, too?

We're invited here from week to week. That invitation to come and dine came only once. This comes every week. Does that make this mean less? I tell you, it makes it means more!

There were only eleven men about the fire that day. The invitation to this supper has been extended to hundreds of us here today and to millions around the world. Does that make it mean less? I tell you, it makes it mean more!

Because the kiss of your child comes often, does it mean less? Because the handclasp of a friend or the embrace of a mate comes often, does it mean less? Because we have this opportunity week by week, does it mean less than that invitation so long ago? It is Christ who invites us here to come and dine.

I once heard a minister say, "As we begin to worship we want to invite God to be our honored guest." Of course, there is a sense in which that is true. There is also a sense in which the opposite is true. God invites *us* to be *His* honored guests, just as He did long ago.

Those eleven men who had their breakfast by the sea had all grown up in the same little region of Galilee. Among the twelve only one, Judas, was not from Galilee. By the time of this text, he was dead. These were men who had known each other in their childhood and in their youth.

On the other hand, we come from different parts of the country and perhaps from different parts of the world. There was a time when we didn't know each other. There was a time when we didn't love each other. There was a time when we didn't care for each other. Now we do know each other and we do love each other and we do care for each other. Doesn't that make the Lord's supper richer for us than it was for them? How marvelous is that invitation, "Come and dine."

That first Lord's supper in the upper room was celebrated in the dim light of the moon. This breakfast by the sea is in the half-light of dawn. We have come here today in the full, broad sunlight of midday. Does that diminish our worship?

We who speak the English language are blessed because our word "sun" and our word "son" sound the same. We come here in the bright sunlight of midday to talk about the spiritual "sonlight" of the Son of God and it enriches our worship.

When the Lord's supper was first given, the cross was still in the future. The blood of Jesus had not yet been shed. His hands had not yet been pierced. Now we look back to a cross that has been raised, blood that has been shed, and hands that have been pierced. Our worship is all the richer for it. What an opportunity we have when this table is spread and Jesus says, "Come and dine."

It is at His invitation that we come. We do not come to Communion at my invitation. We do not come to Communion at the invitation of the church. We come to Communion at His invitation. But there is another invitation yet to be extended. The Bible speaks of it in the book of Revelation.

Blessed and holy are they who are invited to the marriage supper of the Lamb.

A wedding in Jesus' day was quite different from a wedding in our own day. It began when all the friends of the groom went to his house. They formed a parade. Then all the friends of the bride went to her house. They started a parade. Somewhere in the city, the two parades met. They went to the place where the wedding supper was held. There the festivities began.

The Bible says that someday the Lord is going to form a procession in Heaven with all His holy angels. He's the bridegroom. We're going to form a procession here on earth with all the saints. We're the bride. The two processions are going to meet in the air. Then we'll all go to the marriage supper of the Lamb.

I want to be there. Not everybody likes to go to weddings. That's one I don't want to miss.

There have been some splendid weddings in the world. The most lavish wedding I've ever read about occurred in Innsbruck, Austria. The daughter of the Empress of Austria and King Frederick I, who was to become the Holy Roman Emperor, were married. The two most powerful royal families in Europe were united. They created for the occasion a thing called "The Golden Roof."

I had read about it long before I got to go to Innsbruck, Austria, and I was really anxious to see it. It was something of a disappointment. I don't know what I expected to see, but I certainly expected to see a lot more than I saw. The golden roof is not much more than a kind of awning that extends out over a balcony and I'm not even sure that it's real gold. Even if it is real gold, they use that to pave the streets of Heaven. It's not too impressive. But it's the best the world has to offer.

That wedding supper described in the book of Revelation is one I want to attend.

I often sit down with couples to help plan their weddings. It always amuses me that they assume everyone they have invited will attend. They'll talk about how big the hall needs to be and how many people are going to be there. They always assume that everyone they have invited will come. I know better!

But everyone who is invited to this wedding will come. Jesus told a parable once about a man who gave a wedding feast. He said that many of the people who were invited didn't come. The host wanted the hall to be filled. So, he sent his servants out into the street to gather up people and bring them in so the hall would be full. That's not a parable of the future! That's a parable of the present.

Then Jesus gave a parable of the future. Perhaps it's the second act of the same parable. He said there was a man who came in without a wedding garment. It wasn't that he didn't have a wedding garment. He purposely didn't put it on to show his contempt for the bride. They threw him out. That's a parable of the future.

Two things are certain about the wedding supper of the Lamb. One is that nobody is going to be there who didn't get an invitation. The other is that nobody is going to be there who's not prepared to go.

There's a little chorus that I've heard since childhood. It always meant a lot to me.

Into my heart,
Into my heart,
Come into my heart, Lord Jesus.

I wonder if today we might just turn that little chorus upside down? If we do, we'll have a more accurate picture of what it means to become a Christian. Let's imagine that it is not us but Christ who sings it.

Into My heart,
Into My heart,
Come into My heart, says Jesus.
Come in today,
Come in to stay,
Come into My heart, says Jesus.

Here Comes the Bride

The last words Christ spoke to anyone on earth He spoke to John on the island of Patmos as recorded in Revelation, 22: "Surely, I come quickly." Twice before in that chapter Jesus said, "Behold, I come quickly." Certainly, the last words Christ ever spoke constitute a significant text.

The book of Revelation is filled with predictions, but the first and the last are a prediction of the second coming. It is filled with promises, but the first and the last are a promise of the Lord's return. It is the only book in the Bible that begins and ends with a prayer—and it is the same prayer: "Even so, come."

He Will Be Seen

Revelation 1:7 says, "Behold, he cometh with clouds; and every eye shall see him, and they also which pierced him . . ."

Not everyone saw Him when He came the first time. Only those fortunate ones who lived at just the right time and just the right place saw Him then. The next time, however, *every eye* shall see Him. His first coming was announced. His second coming has been announced. His first coming was believed by some but rejected by many. The news of His second coming is believed by some, rejected by many. Then many missed seeing Him; but the next time every eye shall see. Then many did not acknowledge Him, but in the time to come *every tongue* shall confess. Then many did not accept Him; but the next time *every knee* shall bow. Think of it! Every eye! Every tongue! Every knee!

Those alive at the Lord's return will all see Him. Those who have fallen asleep in Jesus will see Him (1 Thessalonians 4:13-18). His enemies will see Him (Revelation 1:7). He will be seen.

He May Come Soon

Some would be more definite than that, but Scripture does not justify it. How shall we explain the word "quickly"? Peter talked about that problem and reminded us that a day is with the Lord as a thousand years and a thousand years as a day. Jesus just left day before yesterday! What's your hurry?

Quickly means suddenly. The Bible says, "as a thief in the night." The thief does not ring your doorbell—he bursts into your room. The Bible says "as lightning." We predict eclipses of the sun and moon, but no one says, "You may see lightning flash at 10:38 p.m. Saturday." "In the twinkling of an eye," says the Bible, Christ will come. It doesn't take long to blink your eye. That means that from the time Christ leaves Heaven until He arrives on earth will be only an instant.

He may come tomorrow. He may delay ten thousand years. I don't know. You don't know. Jesus said the angels didn't know. Just as the thief gives no sign of his coming, so our Lord will give none.

You can get a timetable for the train, the plane, or the bus; but there is no timetable for our Lord's return. Some thought it would be in the lifetime of the apostle John, but they were wrong. William Miller thought it would be in 1843, but he was wrong. He then found his mistake and changed the date to 1844, but Christ didn't come then either.

Piazza Smith studied the Great Pyramid and said He would come in 1881. He didn't. Dimbelby said He would come in 1898. He didn't. Thousands gathered at Nyack, New York to await His coming in 1908. He didn't come. Charles T. Russell was sure it would happen in October, 1914. It didn't. His successor moved the date to 1936, but again, nothing happened. In spite of those two errors, the sect of Jehovah's Witnesses managed to survive.

The world is filled with waiting rooms. We wait in hospitals and in doctor's offices, in airports and depots. All of life is a waiting room. This whole earth is a waiting room waiting for the return of our Lord. And no one knows when He is coming.

He Will Come Surely

That word "surely" is found on the last page of the Bible and on the first. In Genesis, God said of the forbidden fruit, "In the day ye eat thereof ye shall surely die." Did it happen? Are we still living in Paradise? Can anybody say that this world with its disease, its disasters, its sin, and its death, is the Garden of Eden? As certainly as that "surely" came to pass, so will this "surely" come to pass.

He said, "I go to prepare a place for you. And if I go . . . I will come again." Study that text backward. If Jesus is not coming, then He has not prepared a place for us. And the only place for us is here, on this earth, with all its trials and difficulties. Or look at Revelation 22:12: "Behold, I come quickly; and my reward is with me." If He is not coming then there is no reward. Sin must go forever unpunished. Virtue must go forever unrewarded. Service must go forever unnoticed. The books of life must go forever unbalanced.

Or look at Revelation 1:8: "I am Alpha and Omega, the beginning and the ending, saith the Lord, which is, and which was, and which is to come, the Almighty." As surely as He was, He is to come. Does anyone doubt He once was here? It is equally certain He will come again. He bases it on His own divine nature. "I am Alpha and Omega." This is no fringe doctrine on the periphery of our faith. To strike at the doctrine of the second coming is to strike at Christ himself. If He is not the end then He is not the beginning. If He is not the last then He is not the first.

I hear the voice of God in Eden in that mysterious verse that means, "He's coming!" I hear prophets, patriarchs, and psalmists all say, "He's coming!" I hear children shouting as they pad down the dusty lane of a Galilean village, "He's coming!" I hear the crowd that looked out from Jerusalem to see His triumphal entry as it wound down the slopes of Olivet. As they run to join it, I hear them shout, "He's coming!" I hear the witness of the church from age to age, "He's coming!" I hear His own witness, "Surely I come quickly."

The first time He came as a babe. The next time He comes as a bridegroom. The first time He came with a song. The next time He comes with a shout. The first time He came to save. The second time He comes to judge. What preparation are you making for His return?